Regional Rural Banks and Rural Development

Dr. Y. Subbarayudu
Prof. P. Mohan Reddy

SERIALS PUBLICATIONS
NEW DELHI (INDIA)

First Published – 2011

ISBN: 978-81-8387-435-9

Published by

SERIALS PUBLICATIONS
4830/24, 1st Floor, Ansari Road
Darya Ganj, New Delhi-110002 (India)
Phone : 23245225. Fax : 91-11-23272135
E-mail: serials@satyam.net.in

Regional Rural Banks and Rural Development

Contents

CONTENTS

FOREWORD

India is basically an agricultural country and the study of rural development has attracted attention of the economists, planners and social scientists in India. Agricultural development is crucial because it provides economic sustenance and builds up a strong industrial base. RRBs are the great source and tool of economic planning geared to attain the goal of rapid rural development. The importance sof rural banking in economic development of a country cannot be overlooked as village economy forms the backbone of Indian economy. Without the upliftment of rural economy as well as rural people of our country, the objectives of economic planning cannot be achieved. In fact, the real growth of Indian economy lies in the emancipation of rural masses from acute poverty, unemployment, and socio-economic backwardness. Keeping this in view, various important plans and programmes of rural development have been conceived and implemented by the government of India since the commencement of first five-year plan. It is evident from a study of these programmes that the desired objectives could not be achieved because of lack of accessibility to cheaper credit to the rural poor.

The RRBs were established with a view to develop the rural economy by providing cheaper credit and other facilities, particularly to small and marginal farmers, agricultural labourers, artisans and small entrepreneurs, and for matters connected therewith and incidental thereto. The present research study focuses on rural finance by Rural banks, particularly the Rayala seema Grameena Bank(RGB), Kadapa. Though based on a case study, it brings out the role of RGB in financing the rural poor and the impact of bank finance in the development of rural areas. The study reveals, how far the RRBs particularly the RGB could succeed in cultivating the habit of savings and banking among the rural masses and how the RRBs have been instrumental in channelizing the funds into most needed and productive purposes such as agricultural and its allied activities and rural artisans by giving required priority to the scheduled castes and scheduled tribe people in the rural India and helped in reducing the dominance of money lenders. The study also focused on the problems such as delay in sanctioning and disbursement of loans, inadequate amount of loan, rigid terms and conditions, poor cooperation from the bank officials, inadequate technical and legal assistance, wrong identification of borrowers, political interference in selection of beneficiaries and the like encountered by both beneficiaries and banks.

The authors conducted relevant analysis of the performance of RRBs in advancing loans to the rural people in India. The observations of the study will be helpful for the bankers as well as the Government to take suitable measures for regulating the existing deficiencies and to the provisions of requisite financial help to the needy rural people. The book will also be of immense use to the researchers, academicians, students, bankers and policy makers.

Dr. C. Siva Rami Reddy
Professor of Commerce & Registrar
Yogi Vemana University, Kadapa

1

Introduction

Rural development is a driving force of the entire development process and lies at the heart of the national development. Rural development does not mean mere development of rural areas rather it is concerned with the development of rural people to dispel ignorance and poverty and assist the process of creating self-reliant and self-sustaining healthy modern communities. It is associated with three main aspects such as[1]:

- improving the living standards of population;
- ensuring mass participation in developmental activities; and
- making the development process self-sustain.

In a broader sense, rural development is a comprehensive programme of activities which includes agricultural growth, setting up of economic and social infrastructure, fair wages, housing and house sites for the landless, village planning, public health and functional literary communications[2].

The Government of India has formulated and implemented special areas and specific programmes that could benefit the weaker sections of the society. To reach the neglected and weaker sections, programmes were drawn up for small and marginal farmers and agricultural labourers like Small Farmers Development Agency (SFDA.) and Agency of Marginal Farmers and Agricultural Labourers (MFAL) in order to identify the poorest families and help them to improve economically. The Antyodaya Programme was also taken up on the same line. Further, as two-thirds of the people live in their district regions, Integrated Tribal Development Programme (ITDP) was also taken up. Again, with a view to identifying the requirements of the families of weaker sections as well as the local potentialities and the infrastructure, a wide ranging programmes under the banner 'Integrated Rural Development Programme (IRDP) has also been undertaken. Likewise, those areas which are affected either by less rainfall or by drought have been recognized and a special programme called—Drought Prone Area Programme (DPAP) has been implemented. Furthermore, some other such special programmes viz., Crash Scheme for Rural Employment (CSRE), Command Area Development Programme (CADP), Pilot Programme, Desert Area Development Programme, the Food for Work Programme, National Rural Employment Programme and Job Guaranteed Schemes have been taken up to improve the welfare of the weaker sections[3].

RURAL DEVELOPMENT – A CONCEPTUAL VIEW

Rural development has been the slogan of almost all political parties and one of the major objectives of Five-Year- Plans since independence. The political parties, planners and policy-makers have realised that rural development can no more be a vote fetching slogan but it is the key issue for national progress. Therefore, the planning commission, in the Five-Year- Plan documents has defined rural development as "the economic betterment of people as well as greater social transformation." The document further emphasises that economic betterment is possible through the development of agriculture and allied activities and social transformation through improvements in health, education, drinking water, energy supply, sanitation and housing.

Several opinions were expressed concerning the concept of rural development and different interpretations were given by distinguished scholars. According to Sanders, rural development provides a large umbrella under which all the rural people can be brought together for channelising their efforts for their own betterment[4]. The Ahsridge Conference on Social Development defines rural development as movement designed to promote better living for all in the whole community with the active participation and an initiative of the community[5].

In the words of Ensminger, rural development seeks to involve a process of transformation from traditionally oriented cultures towards an acceptance and reliance on science and technology[6]. Lele defines rural development, as an improvement in the living standard of masses of low-income population residing in rural areas and making the process of self-sustaining[7]. According to Giriappa, rural development involves developing rural economy so as to raise the standard of living of those rural people who are poor and require upliftment[8]. In fact, rural development involves a process wherein the rural society as a whole moves from one step ahead and, thereby enhancing its social and economic standards.

To sum up, rural development implies a process to provide an opportunity for decent living to the masses of low income population residing in rural areas on self sustaining bases. It embraces all those programmes that touch all levels of human living i.e., agriculture and allied activities, health, communication, supplementary employment through village and small scale industries, housing and social welfare.

OBJECTIVES OF RURAL DEVELOPMENT

The main objectives of rural development are enlisted below[9]:

- to secure the fullest development of all the material and human resources of the rural areas;
- to maximise production in agriculture and allied activities in rural areas through the use of modern technology and improved scientific knowledge;
- to raise the socio-economic status of those families who have adopted agriculture as their profession;
- to lead rural people from the chronic under-employment to full employment;
- to generate maximum possible employment opportunities in rural areas, especially for the weaker

sections of the society through the establishment of rural industries with emphasis on village and cottage industries so as to enable them to improve their standard of living; and

- to provide certain basic amenities like drinking water, electricity, especially for productive purposes, roads connecting villages to marketing centers and facilities for health care, education and the like.

In a nutshell, rural development aims at all-round development of rural economy with more emphasis on socio-economic amelioration of rural people.

ASPECTS OF RURAL CREDIT

Indian economy is rural economy. Nearly four out of five Indians live in the rural areas and within the rural India itself, five out of every six are dependent on agriculture[10]. Agriculture with its allied activities contributes as much as 41 per cent to national income and it provides food-grains as well as vital raw-materials to agro-based industries like cotton textiles, jute textiles, sugar, edible oils and the like[11]. Rural development is a strategy to improve the economic and social life of a specific group of people, the rural poor including small and marginal farmers, tenants, landless and the poorest among those who seek livelihood in the rural areas. The basic aim of rural development in our country is, therefore, to transform the socio-economic life of the country's rural population living below the poverty line in the rural areas[12].

An old French proverb says, Credit supports the farmers as 'the hangman's rope supports the hanged'. But, if credit is sometimes fatal, it is often indispensable to the cultivators. Credit is the confidence reposed in a person, enables him to obtain from another for the temporary use of a thing or value. It is obvious that credit is an ability to get loan from some individual or agency. The persons who obtain finance with the help of this capacity to influence the lender may not have any productive asset. Consequently, credit is the confidence creating power of the borrower. One commonly gets the operational credit by convincing a lender that the amount with some interest will be repaid by the specified time limit. Put in a different way, credit is an arrangement between a borrower, who takes some money for productive investment and a lender who deploys his capital for earning some interest[13].

In the context of small farmers, credit means short term credit. As the small farmers live below or on the poverty line in India, they are not in a position to avail themselves of long term loans. In the Indian context, it is considerably low and in making any agreement, the borrower is dictated by the lender because the farmer is weak and has very limited alternatives. Small farmers' credit is, therefore, the money lending and borrowing business. Further, it is essentially an operation of securing money from one source or the other by creating the confidence that the amount of loan would be invested in productive operations and that the lender will get back the loan with some extra as per agreement[14]. Thus, agricultural credit reflects agricultural situation in a different way and is dependent upon agricultural yields and related matters.

Agencies for Rural Credit

Credit is considered as an important instrument for agriculture and rural development and is available to the villagers from two types (see Fig 1) of broad sources, viz., the institutional and non-institutional.

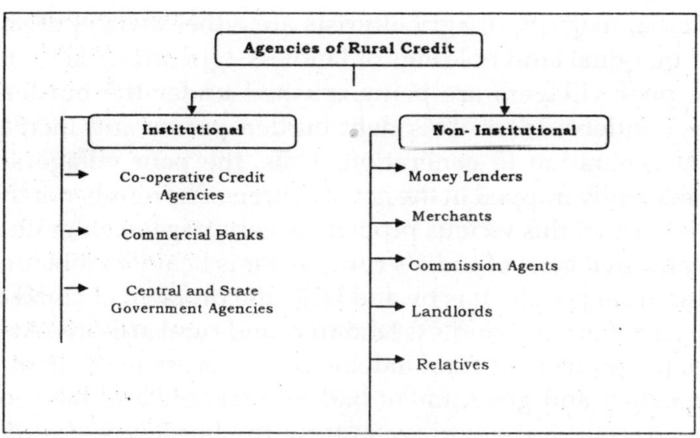

Figure 1

The institutional sources include co-operative credit agencies, commercial banks, Central and State Government agencies while the non-institutional sources consist of mainly money lenders, merchants, commission agents, landlords, relatives and the like. Due to the nature and direction of public policy in the first three Five-Year Plans, non-institutional agencies occupied a dominant place in the rural credit structure. According to the All India Rural Credit Survey Report, the share of institutional agencies, comprising of the Government, the co-operatives and the commercial banks in financing the borrowings of the rural households was 7.1 per cent in the year 1951-52, whereas the corresponding share of private money lenders alone was as high as 68.6 per cent[15].

Number of enquiries and studies have brought out from time to time regarding the exploitative character of the money-lenders. As regards the money-lenders' rate of interest, it is difficult to state precisely the different rates charged in different parts of India. As pointed out in the report of the Expert Committee on Consumption Credit, the money-lender also exploits the poor borrowers through advance contract for tied sale of output only through him which in turn he gets output at lower price than the borrower could have obtained, if he sells output directly in the market.[16]

Rural Indebtedness

In India, majority of agriculturists are either owners of small and marginal land holdings or landless agricultural labourers. The poor villagers are being crushed under the burden of heavy indebtedness. This debt burden passes and increases from generation to generation. Thus, the poor villagers are permanently trapped in the net of usurers. The number of those in the grip of this vicious problem is very large. As a matter of fact, the evil facet of India's rural sector is heavy indebtedness of the rural people. It is by and large the problem of small and marginal farmers, landless labourers and rural artisans. At one time the problem of rural indebtedness has assumed alarming proportion and government had to intervene and take some steps to relieve the borrowers from the burden of past debt, also make some provision to provide loan for their agricultural operation and even to meet their consumption needs. Agricultural borrowers, thus, would not be compelled to go to money-lenders for borrowing funds either for their consumption needs or productive purposes[17].

Causes of Rural Indebtedness

Against the aforesaid background, it would be interesting to mention the causes for rural indebtedness. There are several causes responsible for rural indebtedness. The major causes for indebtedness are[18]:

Vicious Circle of Poverty

The low level of income with hardly any savings, the poor villagers have no option but to go for loans for consumption as well as for production purposes. It becomes difficult for small and marginal farmers, rural artisans, and landless labourers to repay their loans and thus, the debts go on accumulating.

Unscrupulous Money Lenders

The loans contracted by the rural poor not only perpetual but also increase because of the unscrupulous usurers. Their rate of interest is very high. They give loans by getting the thumb impression of the ignorant, illiterate and helpless poor borrowers on blank paper. They do not issue receipt for payment of interest or installments paid. They also manipulate in accounts so that the poor farmers can never get out of the clutches of money lender.

Social and Religious Requirements

The social and religious values overrule the economic considerations of conservative and traditional minded rural folk. The villagers incurred heavy unproductive expenditure on religious social customs like birth, marriages and death ceremonies. They often borrow from the unscrupulous money-lenders and get permanently caught in the clutches of money-lender.

Litigations

There are inter-family and intra-family disputes, which often force the villagers to go to the courts. To meet this expenditure credit is required.

Other Causes

The small and marginal farmers are forced to pay their rent and land revenue by taking loans. Their other expenses like medical help, purchase of utensils, clothes, ornaments and the like are met from these loans.

RURAL CREDIT REQUIREMENTS

Credit is the king-pin of economy's progress. It is the basic need for every sector of the economy and rural sector is no exception to this phenomenon. The major objective of planning in India, has been to improve the quality of life and to raise the standard of living of the rural people. The realisation of this goal depends, to a large extent, on the development of the rural sector as 70 per cent population reside in this sector. Availability of credit is the constraint in the tempo of rural development. Credit is needed in all the sectors such as agriculture, industry, trade, transport and various services for their day-to-day activities and also for growth and progress. The following are some important requirements of rural credit[19]:

Production Credit

Most of the credit requirements are linked to the productive purposes. An agriculturist requires credit to buy seeds, fertilizers, water, pay wages to workers and the like. These farm expenses are of recurring nature and are related to agricultural operations. Since farmers' economy is of subsistence and having no savings, they require credit to carry out productive activities.

Investment Credit

The investment on permanent additions and improvement of farm assets as digging wells, fencing the land and clearing marshy can be termed as productive investment. The farmers require credit for making permanent improvements of land which can be termed as investment credit.

Consumption Credit

The rural poor have chronically deficit budgets and have no savings. They require credit to meet their consumption such as purchasing of food grains, clothing and utensils, meeting medical expenses, repairing the houses and celebrating social and religious ceremonies like birth, marriages and death.

The rural credit is also needed to pay the premium to their insurance, purchase of gold, silver ornaments, shares/bonds and the like

FACETS OF PRIORITY SECTOR

The banking institutions are the custodians of private savings and powerful instruments to provide credit. They mobilise the resources of the country by accepting deposits and channelise them for industrial and national development by granting advances[20]. Credit is an important instrument required for national development and it should be utilised according to the national priorities[21]. Before nationalisation, there were complaints that commercial banks in India were diverting their advances to the large and medium scale industries and big business houses. The sectors demanding priority such as agriculture, small scale industries and exports were not receiving their due share. This was one of the chief reasons for the imposition of social control by amending the Banking Regulation Act with effect from 1st February 1969[22].

Until the mid sixties, the beneficiaries of bank credit were the people having direct or indirect influence over administration of banks. Hence agriculture, small-scale industries and other priority sectors failed to get the required bank credit in spite of their importance in the country's development planning. Towards the end of 1965, a beginning was made to mould the credit policy of the commercial banks so as to make it consistent with the planning policies. In accordance with this prospective, "Credit Autherisation

Scheme" was introduced in November 1965. Later on the scheme of social control over banking was introduced, under which banks were required to allocate bigger amount of credit to priority sectors[23].

The concept of the priority sector was first formulated in 1972 on the basis of the report submitted by the Informal Study Group on statistics relating to advances to priority sector by RBI in May 1971[24]. A more detailed examination of various categories and sub-categories of borrowers, now being classified as priority sector, was undertaken by the Krishna Swami Working Group in 1980. The group evolved the concept of weaker sections within the segment of priority sector. In the year 1982, the RBI set up Working Committee under the Chairmanship of Sri. A. Gosh to examine the scope for modifications in the definition of the priority sector and to review the then existing targets and sub- targets with special reference to the needs of the weaker sections[25]. While no change was considered necessary by the group, in the overall composition of the priority sector, modifications were proposed in the definition of some of the components to ensure that the thrust was towards financing the small borrowers.

Initially, there was no specific target fixed for priority sector lending. The banks were advised to increase the share of priority sector advances to 40 per cent of the total advances by March 1985. Reserve Bank of India prescribed lower rate of interest for the priority sector advances when compared to traditional advances and minimum lending rate ceiling is also not applicable to these advances in specified cases. Inclusion of particular category into the priority sector confers certain specific advantages over other borrowers in all respects[26].

Segments of Priority Sector

The priority sector at present includes the following segments:

- Agriculture
- Small Scale Industries (SSIs)
- Road and Water Transport Operations
- Retail Trade

- Small Business
- Professional and Self Employed
- State Sponsored Organization for Scheduled Caste (SCs)/Scheduled Tribes (STs)
- Self Help Groups (SHGs)

Agriculture

Financing for agriculture purpose is of three types, i.e. Short term, medium term and long term loans. Short term loans are given to farmers for raising crops. In addition, advances up to Rs 1 lakh will be provided to farmers against hypothecation of agriculture produce for a period of not exceeding six months. Medium and long-term loans are given to farmers for purchasing of agriculture implements, farm machinery, plough animals, trucks, bullock carts, tractors, trailers and other transport equipment. Loans are also given for constructing, deepening and cleaning of surface wells, bore-wells, purchase and installation of turbine pumps, construction of lift irrigation projects, conversion of dry land into wet irrigated land, development of farm drainage, construction of farm buildings, bullock sheds, farm stores, construction of warehouse, and cold storages.

Small Scale Industries (SSIs)

Small Scale Industrial units are those engaged in the manufacture, processing or preservation of goods and whose investment in plant and machinery (original cost) does not exceed Rs.3 crore to be classified under small-scale industry. Advances to industry related to Small Scale Service / Business Enterprises having investment in fixed assets excluding land and building upto Rs.25 lakh and registered as such are also to be treated as advances to SSIs[27].

Road and Water Transport Operations

Advance to small road and water transport operators owning a fleet of vehicles not exceeding six vehicles, including the one proposed to be financed is considered as priority sector advance. The main object of this scheme is to enable the borrowers to have a gainful occupation.

Retail Traders

Advances granted to (i) private retail traders dealing in essential commodities (fair price shop) and consumer co-operative stores and (ii) other private retail traders with credit limit not exceeding Rs.2 lakh are considered under priority sector. Advance to retail traders are extended both for fixed capital needs and working capital needs.

Small Business

Small business would include individuals and firms managing a business enterprise established mainly for the purpose of providing any service other than professional services whose original cost price of the equipment used for the purpose of business does not exceed Rs.10 lakh with working capital limit of Rs.5 lakh or less.

Professional and Self-Employed Persons

Loans to professional persons include loans for the purpose of purchasing equipment, repairing, or renovating existing equipment. Acquiring and preparing business premises, purchase of tools, working capital requirement to medical practitioners, lawyers and solicitors, engineers, architects, surveyors, construction contractors, management consultants or to a person trained in any other art. Self-employed include, persons who holds either a degree or diploma from any institution established, aided or recognized by Government, or a person who is considered by the bank technically qualified or skilled in the field in which he is employed.

State Sponsored Organizations for STs /STs

Advances sanctioned to state sponsored organizations for scheduled castes/Scheduled Tribes for the specific purpose of purchase and supply of inputs to and/or the marketing of the output of the beneficiaries of these organizations.

Self-Help Groups

To begin with Training of Rural Youth for Self Employment (TRYSEM), a number of allied programmes were added over the years such as Development of Women and Children in Rural Areas (DWCRA), Supply of Improved Tool Kits to Rural Artisans (SITRA), and Ganga Kalyan Yojana (GKY). As there are problems in the implementation of these programmes like achieving the individual targets and maintaining the link among these programmes, Government decided to restructure the self-employment programmes. A new programme known as "Swarnjayanti Gram Swarozgar Yojana" (SGSY) has been lauched from April 1999. This is a holistic programme covering all aspects of self-employment such as organization of the poor into Self-Help Groups (SHGs). The SGSY programme is funded by Centre and the States in the ratio of 75:25 respectively.

By launching SGSY , the earlier programmes IRDP, TRYSEM, DWCRA, SITRA, GKY are no longer in operation. The unspent balances, as on Ist April 1999, under these erstwhile programmes, were pooled under the head SGSY and utilised as per the new guidelines[28].

The objective of SGSY is to uplift the poor families (swarozgaris) by ensuring appreciable increase in incomes over a period of time. This objective is to be achieved by inter-alia organizing the rural poor into Self-Help Groups (SHGs) through a process of social mobilization.

Under Swarnjayanti Gram Swarozgar Yojana (SGSY), the beneficiaries are known as Swarozgaris. The swarozgaris can be either individuals or groups. SGSY lay emphasis on the group approach, under which the rural poor are organized into Self- Help Groups. In either case, the list of Below Poverty Line (BPL) households is identified through BPLcensus, duly approved by the Gram Sabha will form the basis for identification of families for assistance under the SGSY[29].

SGSY's approach is to organize the poor stems from the conviction that there is a tremendous potential within the poor to help themselves and that the potential can be harnessed by organizing them. Social mobilization enables the poor to build their own organizations (Self-Help Groups) in which they participate fully and directly and take decisions on all issues concerning poverty eradication. Simultaneously, SHGs have the advantage of the assistance in terms of credit or technology or market guidance.

Social mobilisation is not a spontaneous process; it has to be induced. District Rural Development Agencies (DRDAs) are expected to initiate and sustain the process of social mobilisation for poverty eradication by formation, development and strengthening of the (SHGs). Issues that are key to poverty eradication should become entry points for DRDAs to organise the poor into SHGs. There could be different entry points for different SHGs depending on the local situation. The groups that are formed with thrift and credit as an entry point have demonstrated that the poor can secure greater access to credit and other support services for enhancing their income levels[30].

Stages of SHGs

The following are the steps involed in the formation of SHGs [31]:

Group Formation

The facilitators identify the like mined natural groups which are commonly called 'Affinity Groups'. Identification of such Affinity Group is critical for the progress and success of the Self Help Group. This would require staying with the people for some period to facilitate proper understanding and establish rapport with them. Therefore, while forming groups, facilitators must recognise the natural bonds and affiliations existing within the society.

Group Stabilization

The group takes up internal loaning to the members from their Group Corpus. The groups should save regularly and begin to lend to members. This provides the members with opportunities to acquire the skills to prioritize scarce resources, to assess the strength of each member.

Micro Finance

The Group Corpus is supplemented with Revolving Fund sanctioned as cash credit limit by the Banks or the group could also have access to credit under the Self Help Group-Bank Linkage Programme of NABARD.

Micro Enterprise Development

Group takes up economic activity, of their choice for income generation. This phase would include Entrepreneurship Development as well as Skill Development training of the members of the Group to enable them to successfully implement the chosen activity.

ROLE OF CREDIT IN RURAL DEVELOPMENT

Rural development intends the development of the weaker sections of the society constituted by small farmers, marginal farmers, agriculture labourers, rural artisans, scheduled castes and scheduled tribes. Small and marginal farmers who constitute over 70 per ent of the farming population have little input moblising capacity and risk taking power. Therefore, the main aim of rural development is to bring about a positive change in the life of the weaker sections in rural areas, and it requires, among other things, some supplementary services like credit extension, marketing and the like, in a coordinated way. Credit requirements of rural community particularly of farm producers are on the increase. The rising 'economic consequences, growing conspicuous expenditure even by low income groups, emergence of new land owning class, the advent of new form technology, like poultry, dairying account for the higher demand for credit.

The pattern of indebtedness shows that consumption loans form a larger part of the debt of the rural poor. Loans for medical and educational expenses and ceremonial demands account for a substantial portion of the debt. Production loans are often a small fraction of indebtedness. It has to be remembered that these classes depend for their credit substantially on the moneylender and the rich farmer. Consumption credit is usually taken by the small and marginal farmers to meet the cost of food grain for personal consumption and for payment of wages, till the harvest comes in[32]

The lack of assets coupled with lending policies based on assets, leads to reduced opportunities for the rural poor to avail of credit facilities for improving their incomes. The farmer requires transfer of capital resources to give them a better base for production and the latter requires a more realistic credit policy and comprehensive institutional infrastructure. Thus, a landless labour household has only labour as its resources but it can be used productively only if complementary resources are available. Similarly, the small farmers have assets in the form of their land-holdings but these can generate increased incomes with the application of new farm technology provided there is access to other resources; so also is the case with rural artisans who have the skill but not the capital or other resources. The capital base and the productive capacity of the rural poor will have to be improved and strengthened with the aid of institutional support.

The neglected and the weaker sections of the society need mainly short and medium-term credit provided by the Commercial Banks, Co-operative Banks and RRBs. They are generally not in the need of the long-term credit granted by the Land Development Banks. Short-term credit fulfils the pressing needs of the farmers. Medium-term loans enables the farmers to bring about an improvement in the productive potentialities of lands. Short-term loan is needed to fulfill the pressing needs of the farmers. Medium-term loan enables the farmers to bring about an improvement in the productive potentialities of lands. Short-term loan is needed to fulfill the urgent requirement of agriculture like minor irrigation, land development, purchase of buffaloes and bullocks, agricultural implements, dairy farming, poultry farming, sheep and goat rearing. The farmers also need some non-agricultural credit for supplementing their activities particularly for village and cottage industries, small transport operation, weaving, basket making, and pot making.

The expansion of agricultural credit does not help all categories of farmers to produce more. In the case of the substance farmer, in the early stages of the development, the demand for the consumption credit is also more pressing. This phenomenon arises from the various factors such as poverty reflected in lack of food reserves and the traditional customs of rural life, which often involves heavy expenditure on social and religious emergencies. Further, they also need credit to clear a part of the outstanding debt.

In a country like India, the improvement of farming and other activities at higher productivity and better living conditions of rural people, the poor section of the rural population needs supervised credit for agriculture and other activities. This is an important part of the rural development programmes. H. Belshaw says "Supervised credit is a technical term to describe a particular system of credit aiming at improving both production and family living which co-ordinates credit provision with extension services and aims at effective supervision, but usually goes further in making improved provision for marketing and other ancillary services"[33]

Thus, the weaker sections heavily require the credit for productive and consumption purposes. It is very difficult to draw a clear line between the two because the capital starved section of the population may utilise it in either way depending upon the urgency of the requirements.

REFERENCES

1. Lele, Uma (1975), *The Design of Rural Development Lesson from Africa Washington, D.C*: World Bank Research Publication, p.2.
2. Sing, Baldev (1982), *Rural Development and National Integration, Kurukshatra,* Vol. xxxi, No. 1-15, p.8
3. Sunil Kumar (1990), *Regional Rural Banks and Rural Development,* New Delhi: Deep and Deep Publications, p.138.
4. Sanders, T.H. (1958), *The Community,* NewYark: the Ronald Press Company, p.391
5. A Hand Book of Community Development (1958), London: Her Majesty's Stationery Office, p.2
6. Ensminger, D. (1970), *Rural Development–What is it and its Contribution to Nation Building,* a paper presented at East West

Center's Conference on Integrated Communication for Rural Development, Honulu, p.121

7. Uma Lele (1975), *The Design of Rural Development Lessons from Africa*, Baltimore: John Hopkins Press, p.25
8. Giriappa, S. (1976), *Urbanism and Rural Development*, Bangalore: Institute for Social and Economic Change, p.19.
9. Sandhu, B.S. (1996), *Banking and Rural Development*, New Delhi: Deep and Deep Publications, pp.60-61.
10. Balamohan Das, V. Prabhakar Rao, J.V. and Hrushi Kesava Rao, P. (1991), *Rural Banks and Rural Credit*, New Delhi: Discovery publications, p.1.
11. 1981 Census as mentioned in pigmy, Economic Review (1984), Monthly Economic Journal of Syndicate Bank, Manipal: January, Vol.29, No.6, p.3.
12. World Bank (1975), *The Assualt on World Poverty*, Baltimore: John Hopkins University Press, p.3.
13. Sunil Kumar., *op.cit.*,pp 64-65
14. *Ibid.*, p.66
15. Reserve Bank of India (1954), *All India Rural Credit Survey*, Vol.11, p.167.
16. Government of India, Department of Revenue and Banking, *Report of the Expert Committee on Consumption Credit*, New Delhi: April 1976, Chapter-5.p.25
17. Desai, S.S.M. (1986), *Rural Banking in India.*, Bombay: Himalaya Publishing House, p.159.
18. Priyan, A.K. (1995), *Regional Rural Banks and Rural Development*, Jaipur: Arihant Publishers House, p.9
19. *Ibid.*,p.14.
20. Tannan (1993), *Banking Law and Practice in India*, New Delhi: Orient Law House, p.119.
21. Hand Book of Instructions (1997), Bank of Baroda, Vol. VI-C.1, Baroda, August, p.3
22. Tanan (1993), *op.cit.*, p.119
23. Misra-Puri (1993), *Structure and Problems of Indian Economy*, Mumbai: Himalaya Publishing House, pp.443-444.

24. SBI Manual (1995), State Bank of India, Head Office, Vol.1, Hyderabad, p.115

25. *Ibid.*, p.3.

26. *Ibid.*, p.4.

27. Bedi, H.L and Hardikar, V.K. (1996), *Practical Banking Adavances*, Bangolore: U.B Publishers, p.283

28. Priyan, A.K. (1995), *Regional Rural Banks and Rural Development*, Jaipur: Arihant Publishing House, p.14.

29. *Ibid.*, p.4

30. *Ibid*, p.11

31. Hand book on SGSY (Swarnajayanthi Grama Swarajgar Yojana) (2001), District Rural Development Agency, Govt of Andhra Pradesh, p.25.

32. Reserve Bank of India (1981), "Report of the Committee to Review Arrangements for Institutional Credit for Agriculture and Rural Development (CRAFICARD), Bombay, January, p.18.

33. Balshaw, H. (1959), Agriculture Credit in Economically Underdeveloped Countries, F.A.O., Agricultural Studies No.46, Rome, F.A.O., pp.199-210.

2

Regional Rural Banks: An Overview

Regional Rural Banks (RRBs) are the youngest members of the family of rural credit institutions set up in India. They have been set up specially to meet the credit requirements of the weaker sections of the rural society, whose problems came into sharp focus after the State Government's enacted legislation in the mid-seventies for discharging the debts of marginal farmers from the non-institutional sources. The legislation was enacted in response to the guidelines issued by the Central Government to implement one of the Twenty Point Economic Programmes, viz., to liquidate rural indebtedness, and pass legislation for a moratorium on recovery of debts from landless labourers, small farmers and rural artisans. Such legislation would create a vacuum in meeting both the production and consumption credit requirements of the weaker sections as the traditional sources of credit were expected to dry up[1].

ORIGIN OF REGIONAL RURAL BANKS [RRBs]

It was in the context of these conditions that the Government of India set up Regional Rural Banks (RRBs) during the year 1975, with an avowed object of financing the credit requirements exclusively to the poorer sections in the country side, represents a novel experiment of the Indian banking laboratory[2]. The foundation of the institutional credit structure in rural India was laid with the organisation of Co-operative

Credit Societies at the beginning of this century. The credit needs of the agricultural sector, however, increased rapidly over the years. The co-operative credit structure, which was unevenly developed in different parts of the country, could not keep pace with the growing demand for institutional credit. Commercial banks were, therefore, induced into the field of agricultural credit under the policy of social control over the banks in 1968 and the subsequent nationalisation of 14 major commercial banks in 1969 carried the process further. Rural branches of commercial banks expanded very sharply in the period following nationalisation[3]. But these branches rarely went beyond district or sub-divisional towns. Owing to this reason, Banking Commission (1972) had recommended the establishment of a chain "Rural Banks" in addition to rural branches of commercial banks. Such rural banks, in view of the commission, could come into existence in the following ways[4]:

- conversion of primary co-operative societies into institutions offering full banking facilities;
- establishing subsidiaries of commercial banks; and
- establishing a special type of rural banks sponsored by commercial banks and supported by local participation.

It took the Government three years to decide that a scheme of special rural banks would be necessary but once the decision was taken, things moved quickly. The Government of India appointed the Narasimham Study Group on July 1st 1975[5]. This working group submitted its report on 30th July 1975.

An ordinance was promulgated on September 26th 1975 which was subsequently replaced by Regional Rural Banks Act 1975. According to this Act, the RRBs were set up with a view to developing the rural economy by providing financial help for the purpose of development of agriculture, trade, commerce, industry and other activities in the rural areas, credit and other facilities particularly to the small and marginal farmers, agricultural labourers, artisans and small entrepreneurs and for matter connected therewith and incidental there to[6].

The first six RRBs were established on October 2nd 1975. By the end of 1976, 40 RRBs had been set up. In 1978, the Government setup a Review Committee on RRBs headed by M.L.Dantawala[7]. The Committee considered that the performance of RRBs was good and that the financial results of the working of some of these banks showed that RRBs had the potential and capability to attain financial viability and become a profit making institution in about three to four years. The Committee recommended that steps should be taken to initiate the process of making the RRBs an integral part of the rural credit structure.

CONCEPT OF RURAL BANKING

Rural banks make a new development in the rural credit system tailored to the needs of the people. A rural bank may be said as a primary banking institution set up to serve a compact group of villages generally working as a co-operative or as a subsidiary bank of a commercial bank, functioning or set up in rural area for the purpose of providing banking and credit facilities in that area. The main purpose of rural bank is to provide banking and credit facilities to the rural people[8]. The RRBs have been conceived as:

- an answer to meet the diverse and heterogeneous needs of rural people with different socio-economic and agro-geographical conditions;
- diverted to specific economic and occupational groups., i.e., the small and marginal farmers, agricultural labourers, artisans, and the like; and
- to develop the rural economy by providing not only credit, but other facilities. They are supposed to be a nucleus of rural development progrmme in view of their relatively low cost structure, local ethos and professional management. They are government owned regionally based and rurally oriented banks to supplement the existing institutional credit agencies and not to support them in order to fill up the regional and functional gaps in the rural credit institutional system[9].

Objectives of RRBs

The main objective of setting up of the RRBs is to help or assist the potential rural development of agriculture and economy of the area through providing credit and other facilities to the needful people to the rural area well in time and on reasonable terms, so that they may start some viable production activity. In order to achieve the aforesaid main objectives, the following operational objectives have been conceived:

- to provide a specialized agency which would concentrate its efforts entirely on the extension of credit facilities to small farmers and other small borrowers in the rural area at a relatively very low cost;
- to provide employment to rural educated youth who are properly oriented to look after the needs of the rural community. This type of arrangement alone can ensure a low cost profile envisaged for these rural banks and also to achieve a reasonable level of productivity through relatively more motivated rural youth. These banks will provide job opportunities also by financing subsidiary occupations, reviving rural vocations and life;
- to gradually replacing the usurous moneylender is very significant objective of channelling credit through the RRBs and to reducing the dependence on village moneylender;
- to bridge the credit gaps in rural areas;
- the percentage of population below the poverty line in the rural areas is 51. The RRBs are meant to provide finance to this extremely vulnerable section of the rural society, to mitigate poverty through generation to surplus income and through better planned productive activities. It enables the RRBs to remove the curse of poverty in rural areas;
- the objective of rural banking policy is mainly-to evolve an institutional arrangement to mobilise the

saving of the people even in small amounts and thus to inculcate the habit of saving among the rural masses;

- the RRBs were considered to be a suitable institution to provide needed credit at their door-steps on reasonable terms and conditions so that the weaker sections of people in rural areas could raise their total productivity and their standard of living;
- it is hoped that the RRBs would find their role more rewarding by integrating and coordinating their credit activity with the need for economic and social rural development[10].

Functions of Regional Rural Banks

The various functions of the RRBs are listed as follows[11]:

- to mobilise local savings by means of the various types of deposits;
- to provide short term and medium term credit for agricultural and other purposes to rural producers and long term loans to agriculturists as agent of the land development bank;
- to implement the programmes of the supervised credit tailored to the needs of individual farms;
- to provide various ancillary banking services to local people such as remittance of funds, acceptance of insurance premia, safe- deposit lockers and the like.
- to set up and maintain warehouses;
- to provide assistance in the marketing of agricultural and other products through marketing organisations; and
- generally to help in the over-all development of the villages in its area.

In addition to the banking facilities, it also provides some non-banking facilities to the rural population such as constructing and maintaining warehouses on their own, supplying agricultural inputs and acquiring agricultural and other equipments for leasing it out, providing assistance in the marketing of agricultural and other products.

Management of RRBs

The RRBs are controlled and managed by Board of Directors consisting of nine members (including Chairman). The Government of India and State Government/Sponsor Bank, for a period of not exceeding five years, appoint them. Three Directors are nominated by the Government of India in addition to Chairman, two by the State Government and remaining three by the sponsoring bank. Most of them are officials of the concerned authority.

The first Chairman of RRB was appointed by the Sponsor Bank and the subsequent appointment is made by the Board of Directors of the concerned RRB. The process of recruitment takes place at three levels (a) Branch Manager (b) Field Officer and (c) Cashier-cum-Clerk. The minimum qualification is bachelor degree for managers and officers; matriculation for cashier- cum -clerk[12].

Share Capital of RRBs

The authorised capital of each RRB is Rs. one crore, divided into one lakh fully paid-up shares of Rs.100 each. The issued capital is Rs. 25 lakhs. Of which 50 per cent is subscribed by the Central Government, 15 per cent by the concerned State Government and 35 per cent by the sponsoring commercial banks. As against the issued capital of Rs 1 crore (Rs. 1 crore for each RRB), the paid-up capital of all the 196 RRBs stood at Rs.195.85 crores as on March 2004. Share capital contribution to the extent of Rs. 15 lakhs was to be received by three RRBs (Lakshmi Grameena Bank, Cacher Grameena Bank & Langpi Dehangi Grameena Bank) from state Government of Assam[13].

Share Capital Deposit

As a part of comprehensive restructuring programme, recapitalisation of RRBs was initiated in the year 1994-95. The process continued till 1999-2000 and covered 187 RRBs with aggregate financial support of Rs. 2,188.44 crores from the shareholders (Government of India, Sponsor bank and State Governments). While Government of India and Sponsor Banks have fully released their proportionate share (50 per cent and 35 per cent) of the additional share capital amounting to Rs.1,860.16 crores to all the selected RRBs. Out of total proportionate share (15per cent) of Rs. 328.27 crores of all State Governments, three are yet to release Rs.24.80 crores as their proportionate share in respect of nine RRBs as on 31 March 2004[14].

Geographical Coverage

The Government of India set-up first six RRBs-in Uttar Pradesh and one each in Haryana, Rajasthan, West Bengal and Bihar during the year 1975 by covering 12 districts with 17 branches. By December 1986, the number of RRBs increased to 194 and covered 351 districts in the country, which formed around 80 per cent of the total districts of the country. Uttar Pradesh, Madya Pradesh, Bihar, Rajasthan, Andhra Pradesh and Karnataka have at least 13 Regional Rural Banks each. They accounted for 68 percent of the total RRBs and about 70 per cent branches operating as on December 1986. The number of RRBs established was relatively small in the developed states like Tamilnadu, Maharashtra, Gujarat, Haryana and Punjab. One RRB each in Tripura, Meghalaya, Manipur, Nagaland, Mijoram, Arunachala Pradesh covered the entire state[15].

The progress of RRBs in India is viewed basically from the establishment of RRBs, their branch expansion, average number of branches per bank and total districts covered by RRBs is displayed in Table 1. It is evident that six branches were only established by the end of 1975. This number had advanced to 107 in 1981 and reached to 196 in 1987, and there was no increment in the number of branches from 1987 to date. There was a 32 fold increase in the number of RRBs over a period of decade. The coverage of districts had also improved remarkably from mere 12 in 1975 to 362 in 1987, and stretched to 518 by the end of 2004. The average number of branches per district had jumped from three in 1975 to 34 in 1978, and afterwards a gradual improvement was found upto 74 in 1996. From 1996, a static position has been observed.

Table 1
Progress of Regional Rural Banks in India

Year	*RRBs*	*Total Branches*	*Average Branches per Bank*	*Districts Covered*
Dec 1975	6	17	3	12
Dec 1978	51	1753	34	102
Dec 1981	107	4795	44	182
Dec 1984	173	10245	59	307
Jun 1987	196	13076	66	362
Mar 1999	196	14498	74	486
Mar 2000	196	14301	73	482
Mar 2001	196	14313	73	501
Mar 2002	196	14390	73	511
Mar 2003	196	14433	73	516
Mar 2004	196	14446	73	518

Source: Various Statistical Reports on Regional Rural Banks, NABARD, . Mumbai.

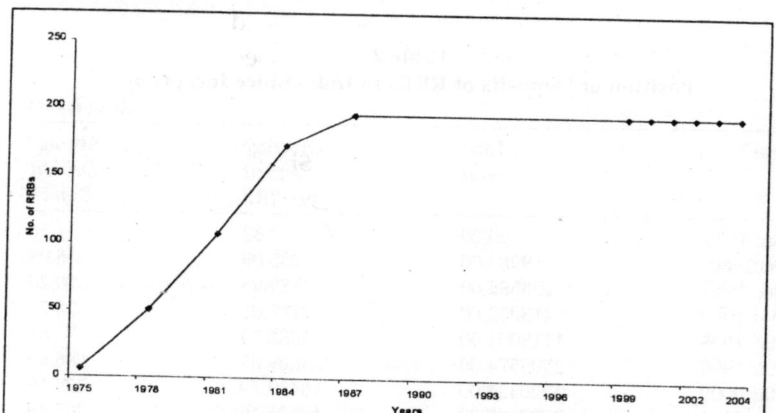

Figure 1: Progress of Regional Rural Banks in India

There has been a marvelous progress in the branch expansion upto 1987. The reason might be to touch the nook and corner of rural areas in the country. It is, thus, deduced that the RRBs have succeeded to a greater extent in taking the banking services to the door steps of the rural masses, particularly to the unbanked rural areas.

Deposit Mobilisation

Mobilisation of deposits is one of the major tasks of the RRBs. It depends upon the saving capacity and saving habit of the people of the area in which the bank is operating. It also depends on the potential of the area concerned and business policy of the RRB. The rate of deposits is depending on the rate of interest offered by the bank. If the rate of interest is high, the amount of deposits also would be more. In addition, the bank policies in mobilising the deposits, the banking habits among the public also play a key role in mobilising the deposits.

It is obvious that deposits of RRBs increased not only in terms of total deposits but also in terms of per RRB and per branch. The total deposits mobilised had swelled to Rs. 1, 28,582.00 lakhs in 1985 from mere Rs. 20.00 lakhs in 1975 (see Table 2). The improvement was 6,429 fold over a period of decade. From December 1990, there had been phenomenal

Table 2
Position of Deposits of RRBs in India Since Inception

(Rs in lakhs)

Year	*Total Deposit*	*Average Deposit per RRB*	*Average Deposit per Branch*
Dec 1975	20.00	3.33	1.18
Dec1980	19983.00	235.09	6.09
Dec 1985	128582.00	683.95	10.20
Mar 1990	415052.00	2117.61	28.74
Mar 1995	1115001.00	5688.78	76.85
Mar 1999	2706574.00	13809.05	186.69
Mar 2000	3220434.00	16430.79	225.19
Mar 2001	3827187.00	19526.46	267.39
Mar 2002	4453915.00	22724.06	309.50
Mar 2003	5009834.00	25560.38	347.11
Mar 2004	5635008.00	28750.04	390.07

Source: Various Statistical Reports on Regional Rural Banks, NABARD, Mumbai.

growth in mobilising the deposits as total deposits had pegged to Rs.56, 35,008.00 lakhs in 2004 from Rs.4,15,052 lakhs in 1990. The average deposits per RRB were Rs.683.95 lakhs in December 1985 as against Rs. 3.33 lakhs in December 1975. It is clear that there had been significant increase from 1990 to 2004.

To be clear, average deposit per RRB had gone up from Rs. 2,117.61 lakhs in March 1990 to Rs. 28,750.04 lakhs by March 2004. There was multifold raise in average deposit per RRB. The average deposit per branch was Rs.10.2 lakhs in March 1985 against only Rs.1.18 lakhs in December 1975. And there was a striking improvement in average deposit per branch after 1985. It had jumped from Rs.28.74 lakhs in 1990 to Rs.390.07 lakhs in 2004. Thus, performance of the RRBs in deposit mobilisation was commandable in the face of competition with the branches of the commercial banks and cooperative banks. It is clear that there is a continuous progress in deposit mobilization and they could mobilize the deposits to the expected level.

Advances

Advance is the important ingredient of banking business. It depends on the potentiality of the area in which the bank is operating and the policy of the bank with regard to credit allocation. The important objective of the RRBs is to touch the doorsteps of each and every neglected section of the society in allocating the loans. Their advances are predominantly confined to the needs of the weaker sections. M.L. Dantawala suggested that 60 per cent of the loans advanced by RRBs should be earmarked for the benefit of small farmers, rural artisans and other rural poor. In respect of remaining 40 per cent loans, there should be a suitable ceiling of each individual loans[16]. The banks generally provide three types of loans; short-term, medium term, and long term loans.

Year-wise position of outstanding advances of RRBs in India is portrayed in Table 3. It is apparent that total outstanding advances registered a remarkable rise from mere

Rs. 10 lakhs in 1975 to Rs. 2,611,385.86 lakhs in March 2004. There was a significant increase continually in aggregate advances over the years under reference. The similar trend could be noticed in average advances per RRB and average advances per branch. For instance, the average advance per RRB had swelled from Rs 1.67 lakhs to Rs 13,323.40 lakhs whereas the average advances per branch from Rs 0.59 lakhs to Rs 180.77 lakhs over the years under study. It may be said that the lending performance of RRB was satisfactory in absolute terms.

Table 3

Position of Outstanding Advances of RRBs in India

(Rs in lakhs)

Year	*Total Outstanding Advances*	*Average Amount per RRB*	*Average Amount per Branch*
Dec 1975	10.00	1.67	0.59
Dec 1980	24338.00	286.33	7.42
Dec 1985	140767.00	748.76	11.17
Mar 1990	355404.00	1813.29	24.61
Mar 1995	629096.00	3209.67	43.36
Mar 1999	1135584.67	5793.80	78.33
Mar 2000	1318424.50	6726.66	92.13
Mar 2001	1581630.46	8069.54	110.50
Mar 2002	1862922.47	9504.70	129.46
Mar 2003	2215784.83	11305.03	153.52
Mar 2004	2611385.86	13323.40	180.77

Source: Various Statistical Reports of Regional Rural Banks, NABARD, Mumbai.

The total finance by RRBs to rural people is divided into two categories–priority sector and non-priority sector. The priority sector includes crop loans, term loans to agriculture, rural artisans, small-scale industries, small business, retail traders, SHGs and the like.

Table 4 gives the statistical details regarding the priority sector advances by RRBs in India. It is evident that the priority sector advances occupied about 75 per cent in the total advances.

Table 4
Priority and Non-Priority Sector Outstanding Advances

(Rs in lakhs)

Year	*Priority Sector*	*Non-priority Sector*	*Total*
1998-99	900272.35 (79.28)	235312.32 (20.72)	1135584.67 (100)
1999-2k	1011122.99 (76.70)	307301.51 (23.30)	1318424.50 (100)
2000-01	1173596.92 (74.21)	408033.54 (25.79)	1581630.46 (100)
2001-02	1376937.52 (73.91)	485984.95 (26.09)	1862922.47 (100)
2002-03	1662522.07 (75.03)	553262.76 (24.97)	2215784.83 (100)
2003-04	2047021.94 (78.39)	564363.92 (21.61)	2611385.86 (100)

Note: Figures in the parentheses represent percentage to total
Source: Various Statistical Reports of Regional Rural Banks, NABARD, Mumbai.

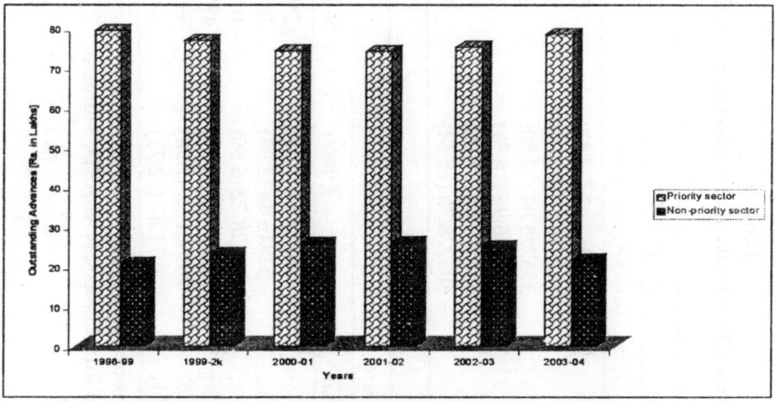

Figure 2: Priority and Non-Priority Sector Outstanding Advances

In the year 1998-1999, the priority sector advances were Rs 9,00,272.35 lakhs (79.28 per cent) out of the total advances of Rs11,35,584.67 lakhs. Though there is a quantitative improvement in the advances to priority sector, a declining trend may be observed up to 2001-02 in terms of percentage. Afterwards it started to rise and 78.39 percent was registered in the year 2003-2004. On an average, the priority sector advances occupied a major chunk in the total advances.

Table 5 shows sector-wise classification of outstanding advances by RRBs in India. In the priority sector, short-term crop loans, term-loans for agriculture and allied activities retail trade occupied more or less equal place. Very less portion i.e. 1

Table 5
Purpose-Wise Classification of Outstanding Advances

(Rs in lakhs)

	Priority Sector			
Year	*Short Term Crop Loans*	*Term Loans (Agri & Allied)*	*Rural Artisans*	*Small Scale Industries*
1998-1999	224019.38 (19.73)	315947.63 (27.82)	54445.23 (4.79)	17656.80 (1.56)
1999-2000	288099.58 (21.86)	332946.87 (25.25)	58413.23 (4.43)	18894.83 (1.43)
2000-2001	369233.61 (23.34)	355723.84 (22.50)	56805.65 (3.59)	25314.65 (1.60)
2001-2002	488267.74 (26.20)	352186.95 (18.91)	67115.80 (3.60)	22483.48 (1.21)
2002-2003	649481.72 (29.31)	376583.65 (17.00)	69463.33 (3.14)	33061.32 (1.49)
2003-2004	766364.65 (29.35)	405778.75 (15.54)	71461.98 (2.74)	43271.16 (1.66)

Contd.

Priority Sector				
Retail Trade	*SHGs*	*Others*	*Non-priorty Sector*	*Total*
249473.77 (21.97)	-	38729.54 (3.41)	235312.32 (20.72)	1135584.67 (100)
260852.08 (19.80)	–	51916.48 (3.93)	307301.51 (23.30)	1318424.50 (100)
278090.45 (17.59)	–	88428.72 (5.59)	408033.54 (25.79)	1581630.46 (100)
298447.39 (16.02)	19092.08 (1.03)	129344.08 (6.94)	485984.95 (26.09)	1862922.47 (100)
326425.11 (14.73)	39505.69 (1.78)	168001.25 (7.58)	553262.76 (24.97)	2215784.83 (100)
360664.15 (13.81)	66509.38 (2.54)	332971.87 (12.75)	564363.92 (21.61)	2611385.86 (100)

Note: Figures in the parentheses represent percentage to total
Source: Various Statistical Reports on Regional Rural Banks, NABARD, Mumbai.

to 5 per cent of total advances to rural artisans, small-scale industries and others may be observed. The share of short-term crop loans was 19.73 per cent in the year 1998-99. It rose gradually and reached to 29.35 per cent out of the total advances of Rs 2611385.86 lakhs in 2003-04. Term loans for agriculture and allied activities registered 27.82 per cent in 1998-99, declined slowly and reached to 15.54 per cent in 2003-04. A declining trend also can be observed in the case of rural

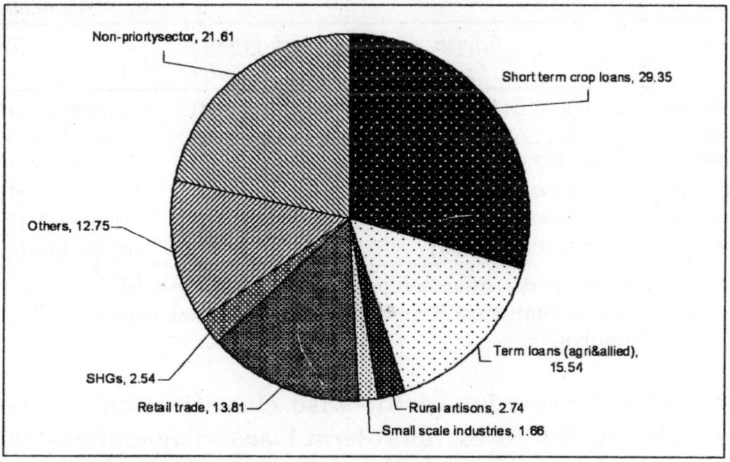

Figure 3: Purpose-wise Classification of Outstanding Advances for Year 2003-04

artisans also. In the year 1998-99, it was 4.79 per cent from the total advances and declined to 2.74 per cent in 2003-04. A meager share was occupied by the small scale industries. It fluctuated between one and two per cent during the period of observation. A downward trend observed in retail trade also. In 1998-99, it was 29.97 per cent and reached to 13.81 per cent in 2003-04. It is observed that short term crop loans and loans for agriculture allied activities occupied the major portion of the RRBs credit. The second important area in the RRBs' credit structure is retail trade. It means RRBs are moving mainly towards achieving the basic objectives set for them.

Classification of priority sector loans issued is shown in Table 6. In the year 1998-99, the percentage of priority sector loans to total loans was 68.47 while non-priority sector was 31.53. In 2003-04, priority sector could register 71.91 per cent and non priority sector 28.09 per cent. It is inferred that the priority sector has got lions' share in the total loans issued. It could receive about 70 per cent of the total loans in almost all the years under the period of study.

Table 6
Sector-Wise Classification of Loans Issued

(Rs in lakhs)

Year	*Priority Sector*	*Non-priority Sector*	*Total*
1998-99	380693.04 (68.47)	175387.75 (31.54)	556080.79 (100)
1999-2k	462642.62 (66.47)	233373.42 (33.53)	696016.04 (100)
2000-01	589477.08 (66.81)	292845.10 (33.19)	882322.18 (100)
2001-02	714269.92 (67.56)	342797.15 (32.44)	1057067.07 (100)
2002-03	884660.78 (69.98)	379439.01 (30.02)	1264099.79 (100)
2003-04	987530.16 (71.91)	385674.50 (28.09)	1373204.66 (100)

Note: Figures in the parentheses represent percentage to total
Source: Various Statistical Reports of Regional Rural Banks, NABARD, Mumbai.

Table 7 provides sector-wise classification of loans provided by the RRBs. Short-term loans to agriculture were more when compared to other categories of loans. In the year 1998-99, these loans registered as 31.70 per cent out of the total loans extended. Gradually, they increased to 44.66 per cent of the loans disbursed. The term loans for agriculture and allied activities had declined from 13.94 per cent in 1999 to 7.59 per cent in 2004.Though there was a declining trend in loans to retail trade, it occupied second place in the priority sector advances provided by the RRBs.

In the year 2001-02, Rs 18012.14 lakhs(1.70per cent) was given to SHGs and it was raised to Rs 50953.62 lakhs i.e 3.71 per cent of the total loans issued. It is inferred that the RRBs have given grave importance to agricultural activities while sanctioning the loans as it is the primary objective of the bank. Next to agriculture is retail trade as there is better recovery of overdue.

Table 7
Purpose-Wise Classification of Loans Issued

(Rs in lakhs)

	Priority Sector			
Year	*Short Term Crop Loans*	*Term Loans (Agri & Allied)*	*Rural Artisans*	*Small Scale Industries*
1998-99	176287.52 (31.70)	77522.09 (13.94)	15191.57 (2.73)	5224.78 (0.93)
1999-2k	241414.75 (34.69)	72878.82 (10.47)	14970.25 (2.15)	6551.11 (0.94)
2000-01	309457.56 (35.07)	87111.33 (9.87)	18083.75 (2.05)	7015.02 (0.80)
2001-02	281161.72 (36.06)	78195.90 (7.40)	19807.17 (1.87)	10671.97 (1.00)
2002-03	483374.08 (38.24)	104531.07 (8.27)	23829.06 (1.89)	13846.26 (1.10)
2003-04	613291.01 (44.66)	104206.05 (7.59)	27621.97 (2.00)	16713.56 (1.22)

Contd.

Priority Sector				
Retail Trade	*SHGs*	*Others*	*Non-priorty Sector*	*Total*
86478.25 (15.56)	–	20018.83 (3.60)	175387.75 (31.54)	556080.79 (100)
99329.45 (14.27)	–	27498.20 (3.95)	233373.42 (33.53)	696016.04 (100)
112272.03 (12.72)	–	55537.39 (6.30)	292845.10 (33.19)	882322.18 (100)
127923.97(12.10)	18012.14b(1.70)	78497.05 (7.43)	342797.15 (32.44)	1057067.07 (100)
142123.06(11.24)	35019.23 (2.77)	81938.02 (6.48)	379439.01 (30.02)	1264099.79 (100)
165315.35(12.04)	50953.62 (3.71)	9428.61 (0.69)	385674.50 (28.09)	1373204.66 (100)

Note: Figures in the parentheses represent percentage to total
Source: Various Statistical Reports on Regional Rural Banks, NABARD, Mumbai.

Credit Deposit Ratio

An increasing credit deposit ratio of the RRBs enables to meet the credit requirements of the rural areas so that the rate of growth in rural areas is accelerated. RRBs are specialised institutions for rural poor. As such credit from the RRBs mainly helps the poor sections of the society for whom credit from all other financial institutions and banks is usually beyond reach. RRBs' credit, thus, goes to reduce the inequality in income between rural and urban areas on the one hand and between the rich and poor on the other.

Table 8
Credit Deposit Ratio

(Rs in lakhs)

Year	*Credit (advances)*	*Deposits*	*C/D Ratio*
1998-99	1135585	2706574	41.96
1999-2k	1318425	3220434	40.94
2000-01	1581630	3827187	41.33
2001-02	1862922	4453915	41.83
2002-03	2215785	5009834	44.23
2003-04	2611386	5635008	46.34

Source: Various Statistical Reports of Regional Rural Banks, NABARD, Mumbai.

Table 8 shows the Credit Deposit ratio of the RRBs in India. Credit-Deposit ratio was registered 41.96 per cent in 1998-99, and declined to 40.94 per cent in 1999-2k. But it started to increase slowly and reached 46.34 per cent in 2003-04. It is observed that though there is a gradual improvement in credit deposit ratio, it did not exceed even 50.0 per cent in any year under the period of study. It is inferred that RRBs could not lend money to the expected levels.

Recovery Performance

Recovery of loans in time is a primary factor for the banks in planning the financing system. If the loan installment becomes overdue, the entire recycling system gets disturbed and weak. Recovery is as important as advance for any financing institution. Timely recovery of loan not only keeps the business running but also benefits the farmers by reducing the load of debt and keeping them eligible for getting fresh loan in future. A good recovery performance leads the bank towards the path of development exercising a positive impact in the areas in which the Bank is operating. A good recovery of loan makes credit flow easier which in turn encourages economic activities, pushing up the rate of economic growth. On the other hand, the poor recovery performance of a credit institution creates many problems such as[17]:

- It makes the credit institutions ineligible to draw refinance from the refinancing agencies.
- It slows down the institutional credit supply which is likely to affect adversely the rural development.
- It adversely affects the confidence of the general public in the soundness of the Banking system.
- In the case of mounting overdues, it would be difficult for the management to make decision with regard to its lending policies, procedures and operations.
- It diverts the staff in the task of recovery instead of devoting time for the development work.

Table 9
Recovery Performance of RRBs in India

(in percentage)

Year	*Short-Term Crop loans*	*Agricultural Investments*	*Allied Activities*	*Overall Agriculture*	*Non-Agricultural Activities*	*Overall Recovery*
1998-99	69.8	52.67	37.48	59.59	61.48	60.43
1999-2k	72.45	54.96	39.38	63.23	65.64	64.25
2000-01	76.34	58.97	40.38	67.20	69.57	68.20
2001-02	76.41	59.55	43.39	68.80	73.16	70.59
2002-03	75.22	59.89	46.72	69.10	75.01	75.52
2003-04	76.76	59.06	46.80	70.59	77.65	73.49

*Source:*Various Statistical Reports on Regional Rural Banks, NABARD, Mumbai

Table 9 shows the purpose-wise recovery performance of RRBs in India. It is obvious that the recovery performance was 60.43 percent in 1998-99 and increased to 73.49 per cent in 2003-

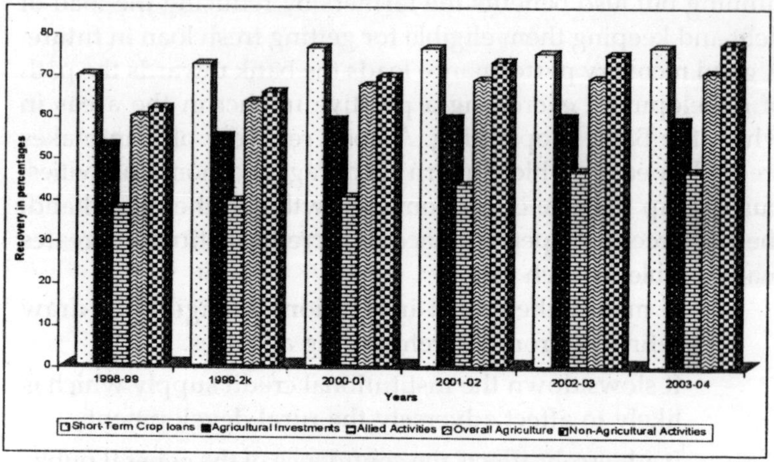

Figure 5: Recovery Performance of RRBs in India

2004. The same trend could be observed in the agriculture and non- agriculture sector also. A good recovery of dues can be seen in short-term crop loans. It was 69.58 in 1998-99 and touched 76.76 in 2003-04. But recovery was poor in agriculture and allied activities. It could not exceed even 50 per cent in any financial year under the period of study. A growth in recovery performance was seen in agriculture investments also. It touched 59.06 per cent in 2003-04 from 52.67 per cent in 1998-99. It is further observed that the recovery is more in short term agriculture loans when compared to agricultural investments and allied activities. But, recovery performance is less in overall agriculture activities when compared to non agricultural activities. Owing to initiation of some measures by RRBs such as implementation of legal actions on defaulters, auctioning of jewelries, availing the services of Vikas Valunteer Vahini Clubs, and the like, RRBs could increase recovery performance during the study period.

Overdues

When a borrower does not pay his due installment amount within the stipulated time then the amount is considered as overdue and the loanee is called a defaulter. Flow of funds is the sine-qua-non of effective banking operation. Bank has no money of its own. It always deals with others' money. Therefore, it is essential for proper financing in borrowing, lending and prompt recovery.

Table 10 gives the statistical information regarding the over-dues of RRBs in India.

Table 10
Overdues Position of RRBs in India

(Rs in lakhs)

Year	*Overdue Amount*	*Outstanding Advances*	*Percentage of Overdues to Outstanding Advances*
1998-99	233101.39	1135584.67	20.53
1999-2k	251492.10	1318424.50	19.08
2000-01	255276.33	1581630.46	16.15
2001-02	282840.20	1862922.47	15.18
2002-03	329547.79	2215784.83	14.87
2003-04	362530.25	2611385.86	13.88

Source: Various Statistical Reports of Regional Rural Banks, NABARD, Mumbai.

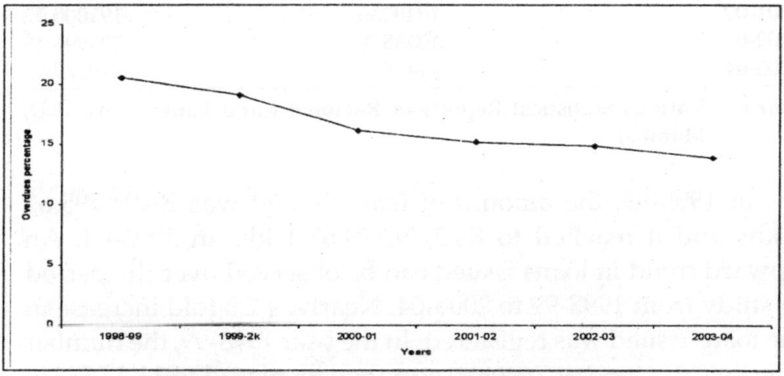

Figure 6: Overdues Position of RRBs in India

It is obvious that outstanding advances had increased from Rs.11,35,584.67 lakhs in 1998-99 to Rs.26,11,385.86 lakhs in 2003-04. The amount of overdue also increased from Rs.2,33,101.39 lakhs in 1998-99 to Rs.3,62,530.25 lakhs in 2003-04. But the percentage of overdues to total outstanding advances had decreased from 20.53 in 1998-99 to 13.88 in 2003-04. It means the RRBs could improve the recovery performance during the study period.

RRBs IN ANDHRA PRADESH

By the end of March 2004, there are 16 RRBs covering 23 districts with 1,170 branches. An analysis on loans and advances, recovery performance and overdue position of RRBs in Andhra Pradesh is carriedout.

Loans Issued

Table 11 gives the information regarding the position of loans provided by RRBs in Andhra Pradesh.

Table 11
Loans Provided by RRBs in Andhra Pradesh

(Rs. in lakhs)

year	*No. of Accounts*	*Loans Issued*
1998-99	752850	93595.62
1999-2k	787628	119273.00
2000-01	935282	148815.47
2001-02	1040636	191000.52
2002-03	1046878	225996.48
2003-04	1147541	279179.67

Source: Various Statistical Reports of Regional Rural Banks, NABARD, Mumbai.

In 1998-99, the amount of loans issued was Rs.93,595.62 lakhs and it reached to Rs.2,79,179.67 lakhs in 2003-04. An upward trend in loans issued can be observed over the period of study from 1998-99 to 2003-04. Nearly, a 2.5 fold increase in the loans issued was registered. In the year 1998-99, the number of accounts stood at 7,52,850 and they increased to 11,47,541in 2003-04. It may be said that RRBs could provide adequate loans to different sectors as loans issued has reported to rise year after year.

Outstanding Advances

Table 12 shows the position of outstanding advances in Andhra Pradesh.

Table 12
Outstanding Advances of RRBs in Andhra Pradesh

(Rs in lakhs)

Year	*No.of Accounts*	*Outstanding Advances*
1998-99	1435189	144799.50
1999-2k	1487577	166198.10
2000-01	1567741	204002.87
2001-02	1736358	246045.83
2002-03	1855063	295354.04
2003-04	2040465	345203.11

Source: Various Statistical Reports of Regional Rural Banks, NABARD, Mumbai.

The outstanding advances had increased from Rs.144799.50 lakhs in 1998-99 to Rs.345203.11 lakhs in 2003-04, registering a two-fold raise. The number of accounts also augmented over a period under observation. It is clear that the lending performance of RRBs in A.P was satisfactory over the period under reference.

Recovery Performance

Position of recovery performance by RRBs in Andhra Pradesh is displayed in Table 13. The overall recovery performance was 61.47 per cent in 1998-99 and it reached to 70.96 per cent in 2003-04. The recovery of loans in agriculture sector was 61.02 per cent in 1998-99. It rose to 67.54 per cent in 2003-04. In the case of non-agriculture sector, an impressive performance could be observed as recovery percentage had strikingly improved from 63.32 to 83.42 over the study period.

Table 13
Position of Recovery Performance of RRBs in Andhra Pradesh

(in Percentages)

Year	*Agriculture*	*Non-Agriculture*	*Overall Performance*
1998-99	61.02	63.32	61.47
1999-2k	62.49	67.23	63.27
2000-01	68.68	71.97	69.28
2001-02	68.03	79.12	70.36
2002-03	66.29	79.59	70.19
2003-04	67.54	83.42	70.96

Source: Various Statistical Reports of Regional Rural Banks, NABARD, Mumbai.

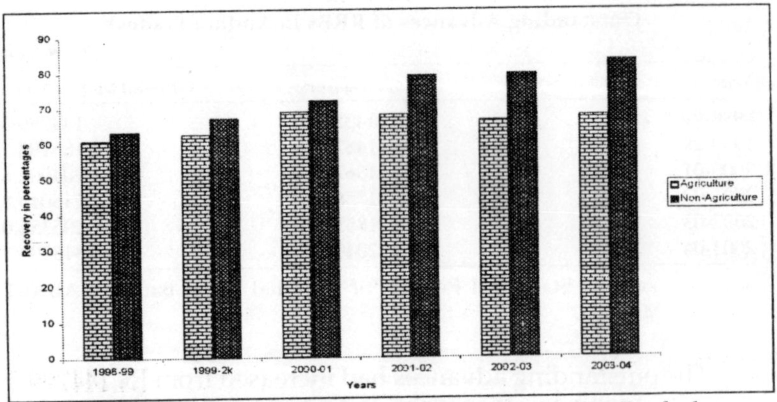

Figure 7: Recovery Performance of RRBs in Andhra Pradesh

It is apparent that the recovery performance was better in non-agriculture sector when compared to agriculture sector. The reason is that cultivation is the only profession for the agriculturists. They are suffering with plethora of problems such as children's education, marriages, ceremonies, health problems and the like. Moreover, agriculture income is the only source to meet their both financial and social problems. Agriculturists are thus, not in a position to repay their dues.

Overdues

Table 14 discloses the details pertaining to overdue position of RRBs in Andhra Pradesh.

Table 14
Position of Overdues of RRBs in Andhra Pradesh

(Rs in lakhs)

Year	*Outstanding Advances*	*Overdue Amount*	*% of Overdues to Outstanding Advances*
1998-99	144799.50	26452.80	18.27
1999-2k	166198.10	34059.00	20.49
2000-01	204002.87	31039.67	15.22
2001-02	246045.83	40126.31	16.31
2002-03	295354.04	47242.21	15.99
2003-04	345203.11	49908.83	14.46

Source: Various Statistical Reports of Regional Rural Banks, NABARD, Mumbai.

It is obvious that the overdue amount had moved from Rs. 26,452.80 lakhs in 1998-99 to Rs. 49,908.83 lakhs in 2003-04. Percentage of overdues to the outstanding advances had slided down from 18.27 in 1998-99 to 14.46 per cent in 2003-04. It may be noted that though the RRBs in Andhra Pradesh could achieve progress in recovery performance, the overdues could not be recovered completely. The major reasons might be inadequate appraisal and follow-up.

Comparative Position - India and Andhra Pradesh

Comparative position of loans issued and outstanding advances by RRBs in India and Andhra Pradesh is portrayed in Table 15 . It is evident that the share of RRBs in A.P. with regard to loans issued in the year 1998-99 was 16.83 per cent and it reached to 20.18 per cent by the end of 2003-04. But in the case of loans outstanding, the share of RRBs in A.P. is reached to 13.21 per cent from 12.74 per cent during the same period. It is inferred that the percentage share of loan issued in A.P. is more than the loans outstanding. It means, the RRBs in A.P. could not recover the loans at expected level when compared to RRBs in India.

Recovery performance and overdues of RRBs in Andhra Pradesh were shown in Table 16. Recovery performance of RRBs both in all-India level and in Andhra Pradesh was more or less remained the same during the period of study. In 1998-99, it was 60.43 per cent in all-India level and 61.47 per cent in Andhra Pradesh. With a gradual increase, it registered as 73.49 per cent and 70.96 per cent at all-India level and Andhra Pradesh respectively.

It is inferred from the data that the RRBs in Andhra Pradesh could increase the rate of percent in recovery when compared to the banks in all over the India. Overdues in Allover the India registered as Rs.233101.39 lakhs in 1998-99 which increased to Rs.362560.25 lakhs in 2003-04. A rise in overdues can be observed in RRBs of Andhra Pradesh. The rate of increase in overdues is more in the banks of Andhra Pradesh when compared to the RRBs in India. It is disheartening to note that the RRBs in Andhra Pradesh have

Table 15

Comparative Position of Outstanding Advances and Loans Provided by RRBs

(Rs. in lakhs)

Year	Outstanding Advances			Loans Provided		
	India	Andhra Pradesh		India	Andhra Pradesh	
	Amount	Amount	%	Amount	Amount	%
1998-99	1135584.67	144799.50	12.74	556080.79	93595.62	16.83
1999-2k	1318424.50	166198.10	12.60	616016.04	119273.00	17.13
2000-01	1581630.46	204002.87	12.90	882322.18	148815.47	16.86
2001-02	1862922.47	246045.83	13.20	1057067.07	191000.52	18.60
2002-03	2215784.83	295354.04	13.32	1264099.79	225996.48	17.87
2003-04	2611385.86	345203.04	13.21	1383204.69	279179.67	20.18

Source: Various Statistical Reports on Regional Rural Banks, NABARD, Mumbai.

failed to collect dues promptly. The performance of Rayalaseema Grameena Bank [RGB] is evaluated in detail in chapter-5 of the present thesis, in order to trace out the reasons at micro level.

Table 16
Position of Overdues and Recovery of Loans in Andhra Pradesh and India

(Rs.in lakhs)

	Recovery Performance in %		*Overdues*	
Year	*India*	*A P*	*India*	*A P*
1998-99	60.43	61.47	233101.39	26452.80
1999-2k	64.25	63.27	251492.10	34059.00
2000-01	68.20	69.28	255276.33	31039.67
2001-02	70.59	70.36	282840.20	40126.31
2002-03	75.52	70.19	329547.79	47242.21
2003-04	73.49	70.96	362530.25	49908.83

Source: Various Statistical Reports of Regional Rural Banks, NABARD, Mumbai.

REFERENCES

1. Chandra Kanth K. Souara (1998), *Regional Rural Banks in India,* New Delhi: Anmol Publications, p.7.
2. Abdul and Dakshinamurthy, M. Rich, O. (1983), Rich *Farmers Garb Benefits Leave Poor Farmers in the Lurch, Yojana,* Vol.27, No.13, July, p.23.
3. Varsheneya, J.S. (1983), *Regional Rural Banks,* State Bank of India Monthly Review, Nov., p.463.
4. Babatosh, Dutta (1979), *Regional Rural Banks,* Report of the Review Committee RBI Bombay, p.103.
5. Ibid. p.104.
6. Harpal Sing (1974), *Regional Rural Banks, Yojana,* Vol.23, Dec. p.13.
7. Varshaneya, J.S. (1983), op.cit, Nov. p.464.
8. Report of the Banking Commission (1972), Government of India, p.490.
9. Sunil Kumar (1990), *Regional Rural Banks and Rural Development,* New Delhi: Deep & Deep Publications, p.134.
10. Chandra Kanth, K. Souara,. op.cit,. p.14.

11. Ibid,. p.16.
12. Sunil Kumar, op.cit, p.156
13. Hand book of Statistics on Regional Rural Banks (2003-04), NABARD, Mumbai, p.15
14. Ibid. p.17
15 Shete, N.B. (1990), *Regional Rural Banks an Analysis, Banking Finance,* April, Vol. III, No.4, 3.
16. Popat, A.N. (1979), *Recommendations of M.L.Dantwala Committee on RRBs,* Bombay, p.10.
17. Sunil Kumar, op.cit,. p.154.

3

Research Design and Methodology

In a country like India, the all-round development of rural areas is imperative as about 80 per cent of the population live in villages. The rural people are living in an atmosphere of absolute poverty, illiteracy, unemployment and under-employment. In the past, no attempt was made by the Britishers to ameliorate the socio-economic conditions of rural poor rather they exploited them. Moreover, their selfish policies had further deteriorated the plight of toiling Indian masses. After independence, the programme of rural development became target of attraction of economists, politicians, and social reformers. It was realized that without the development of entire rural sector, the all-round development of the country would not possible. Rural development is an important tool for bringing about desired improvement in the life of the rural people. It is a strategy designed to improve the social and economic life of a specific group of people. It envisages for bringing about over-all socio-economic development in the country. Moreover, the development and progress of a nation would really mean reconstruction and resurgence of the rural masses of the country. Therefore, the actual growth and development of Indian economy lie in the emancipation of poor masses from the state of poverty in which they have been living for centuries.

STATEMENT OF THE PROBLEM

Among the various infrastructure facilities needed to improve upon the plight of rural masses, the provision of bank credit is certainly sine-qua-non without which rural development becomes difficult. The availability of bank credit is, therefore, one of the strategic inputs for the successful implementation of rural development schemes. But, the institutional finance flowing into agricultural and rural development programmes is significantly low in relation to their share in the national economy. Traditionally, owing to the non-availability of institutional lending agencies like co-operatives and commercial banks, the farmers and other segments used to avail credit from the non-institutional agencies. These agencies, who instead of providing credit facilities, used to exploit them for their selfish ends through the process of charging manipulated high rate of interest and usurp their holdings. At this juncture, co-operative banks have emerged so as to overcome these evils and to provide financial help to the needy villagers. The co-operative banks, however, were not in a position to keep pace with the increasing financial needs of modernisation of agriculture, which started taking place in the late sixties on account of "Green Revolution" besides expansion of rural industrialisation.

In order to ensure that agriculture production may not suffer for want of adequate and need based credit, the introduction of various other financial institutions into the rural credit scene become inevitable. It was this feeling that led to the adoption of "Multi-agency Approach" to the rural finance. The acceptance of this approach has brought the commercial banks into the spectrum of rural finance. With this objective, the Government of India nationalised 14 major commercial banks in 1969, to provide credit facilities to the neglected rural sector. The post nationalisation period in the banking sector has witnessed a substantial amount of resources being earmarked towards meeting the credit needs of the poor. The banking network underwent an expansion phase without comparables in the world. The credit came to be recognized as a remedy for many of the ills of the poverty. Credit packages and programmes were designed basing on the perceived needs of the poor.

Inspite of the tremendous progress in the availability of institutional credit in rural areas in recent years, the contribution of co-operative and commercial banks together never exceeded 40 per cent of the estimated rural credit requirements. Hence, it was felt that more concerted effort was essential to speed up the flow of institutional credit especially to meet the needs of the weaker sections of the rural sector. Consequently, on the basis of recommendations made by the Group headed by Mr. M. Narasimham, the Government of India set-up six Regional Rural Banks [RRBs] on a pilot basis on 2nd October 1975. At present, there are 196 RRBs with 14,443 branch network. The RRBs are intended to develop the rural economy by providing rural credit and other facilities particularly to the small and marginal farmers, agricultural labourers, artisans and small entrepreneurs so as to develop agriculture, trade, commerce, industry and other productive activities in the rural areas. Thus, RRBs emerged as a new dimension in organised banking system. Despite the efforts made by Regional Rural Banks over the past few decades, rural poverty in India continues to be significant. The number of rural poor has more or less remained static and is estimated to be about 244 million. In other words, the underlying objectives of RRBs are laudable, the development in rural areas has not been achieved to the expected levels. Hence, the present study aims at tracing out the reasons for inadequate achievement of rural development.

REVIEW OF LITERATURE

It is proposed to review the literature that exists in the field of bank finance for rural development. In this context, an effort has been made to survey the important studies having impact on the present study. Literature is reviewed both from Books and Articles.

Books

Ghoshal, S.N's "Agricultural Financing in India" deals with the short-term and medium-term credit needs of the farmers. The author feels that despite the existence of co-operatives which were established to make available timely and adequate credit to the farmers, the agricultural development continued to suffer due to lack of credit facilities. He holds that because of the failure of cooperative credit banks are financing this neglected sector[1].

Charan D. Wadhwa's "Rural Bank for Rural Development" is an attempt to evaluate the role of institutional credit in rural development. The author feels that several financial institutions have been established with a view to catering to the financial needs of rural poor. But owing to several reasons like influence of local leaders, complicated banking procedures, lukewarm attitude of banking personnel, corruptions and the like, the poor have not been benefited at all. He emphasises that rural banks must develop simple schemes and co-operative attitude for providing requisite financial help and assistance to the needy rural poor[2]

Pany, R.K., in his book "Institutional Credit for Agriculture in India," attempted to highlight the meaning, need and importance of institutional credit for agriculture. He examined some important things relating agricultural credit like insufficient financial assistance to agriculture, lack of simple and straight forward methods of banking and payment behaviour of agricultural loans by farmers[3].

In the book, "Bank Finance for Rural Development" (edited) Nadiu, L.K., holds that public sector banks have been extending credit facilities to hitherto neglected sectors of the rural economy. They are financing agricultural, small business and small scale industries in a creditable manner to eradicate poverty and unemployment from the rural sector[4].

A study conducted by Narayana, N and Chandrasekhar, G., in six villages in Anantapur district reveals that in the cases of co-operative and commercial banks, more than 80 per cent of credit sanctioned for the purpose of sheep rearing, poultry-forming and artisan activities was directed towards unspecified purposes. This sort of tendency reveals the ineffective and inadequate supervision resulting in non-repayment of loans to banks and thereby aggravating the problem of overdues[5].

Sunil Kumar's study "Regional Rural Banks and Rural Development" is designed to make an indepth enquiry into the performance of RRBs in respect of developing the rural areas and meeting the credit needs of the weaker sections of the population living in the country side. In his work the author examined in detail the problems of rural population, the theoretical aspects of rural development, role of credit in rural development and the like. He opined that the RRBs are acting as catalysts for rural development. His study is mainly confined to the study of sample beneficiaries who come under the purview of Vaishali Kshetriya Grameena Bank (V.K.G.B), Bihar. He concluded that V.K.G.B has financed more to the rich people and thus, the norms and objectives of the bank in respect of lending have not been maintained[6].

The work "Rural Banks and Rural Credit" was developed by Bala Mohan Das, N., Prabhakar Rao, J.V., and Hrushikeseva Rao, in which they have made a joint effort to assess the need of rural credit for the development of rural people. They expressed that the inadequate credit facility provided by the commercial banks and co-operatives emerge the rural banks which meant purely for rural credit. Their study is confined to financial and operational performance of Visakha Grameena Bank, Andhra Pradesh. They concluded that the S.V.G.B has a distinct place with its five points strategy in recovery performance among all the R.R.Bs in the country. However, the low performance in the case of agricultural cash credit and agricultural term loans was due to diversion of agricultural loans for other purposes, ineffective post-supervision of credit, and decrease in agricultural income because of natural calamities. They suggested that so as to register higher rates of recovery, S.V.G.B has to take steps to strengthen effective credit administration for which active co-operation from the staff is to be ensured[7].

Krishanama Raju, S's study "Bank Finance and Rural Development" deals with the credit facilities provided by commercial banks to eradicate the poverty in the rural areas. In his book, he studied the performance of commercial banks' credit on income, employment and asset creation in the agriculture, animal husbandry and tertiary sector[8].

Patnaik, U.C and Mishra, R.N's work "Rural Banking is India", in an attempt to evaluate the role of institutions in financing the agricultural sector. If there is any development of the nation, that is possible only through the development of agricultural sector so that the country to be self-sufficient food grains. He observed that the non-recovery of agricultural credit is a serious problem. His study revealed that out of 300 sample borrowers chosen from sample districts, a larger chunk, and 77 per cent are defaulters. Therefore, he suggested that there should be a lot of care while financing to the agricultural sector as there is mounting overdues[9].

"Regional Rural Banks and Rural Development" by Priyan, A.K., is an empirical study conducted to evaluate the role of RRBs in financing the rural development. In his book, he remarked that rural development is the king-pin of our nation's development. The present study throws light on the rural credit provided by RRBs, the progress of RRBs in India and the impact of bank credit in developing the rural mass. His study is confined to Chakravarthi Grameena Bank, Rajasthan. He found that the bank provided credit facilities to small and marginal farmers. This proves that in true sense their bank is "poor man's bank". He also observed that the bank played a vital role in extending credit facilities to persons belonging to SC/STs in order to bring up these weaker sections above the poverty line[10].

Sandhu, B.S's "Banking and Rural Development" deals with the rural development and different programmes launched for rural development. The main finding of his study is that under the I.R.D.P(Integrated Rural Development Programme), loans were misused by the number of beneficiaries. Some of the sample beneficiaries have utilized the loans to undertake activities other than the main purpose. The basic purpose of providing financial assistance is to provide productive assets to the beneficiaries and to bring about sufficient support in their income so that they may cross the poverty line[11].

Archana Singhal, B.S. Yadav, in his book "Role of Regional Banks in Rural Development", identified that the importance of agricultural development for economic sustenance and to build a strong industrial base. He stated that Regional Rural Banks appeared on the banking map of the country in 1975 have now become the main plank of the organized rural credit structure. In his book, the author explained the extent of availability and utilization of RRB's credit and its impact on rural development. He concluded that the role of RRBs is a great source and tool for economic planning geared to attain the goal of rapid regional development[12].

Pati, A.P's "Regional Rural Banks in Liberalised Environment" reveals the financial viability and profitability of the Regional Rural Banks in the state of Assam. The author tries to identify the important problems associated with the functioning of RRBs. Considering the dearth of research work in this region, this book provides some genuine insight into the functioning of the RRBs in particular and Rural banking in general in the North East region[13].

Acharya Shyama Charan and Mohanty Ashok Kumar , in their book "Operational Analysis-Regional Rural Banks", stated that Regional Rural Banks are an innovative ones in the aspects of objectives, functions, area of operations and its clientele, in the Indian banking scenario. This book provides the existing credit institutions, their strengths and weaknesses in achieving the goals for which they were setup. It identified the necessity of setting up of new institutions called Regional Rural Banks, and analyzed their operations at all India level and in the state of Orissa[14].

Articles

Khemani, C.H, and Balakrishnan, K.V., in their article observed that any credit programme launched for the weaker sections should have consumption credit component as its integral part. In the absence of such an approach, the borrowers will be driven to traditional money-lenders for meeting their urgent consumption needs. As the rates of interest by money- lenders are usurious the repaying capacity despite materialisation of production programmes, is bound to be adversely effected. It is well known that out of any surplus generated, it is easier for the money lender to recover his dues before bank dues are paid[15].

In an article entitled "Rural Banking for Rural Poor" Mishra, H.N., holds the view that the RRBs were established with a view to providing financial help to the rural poor. But the beneficiaries of these banks are mostly the rich farmers and not the small and marginal ones. According to the author, this practice is mainly due to the collusion and corrupt practices indulged in by the bank officials and the influence of local leaders[16].

In an article "Expanding Role of Banks in Rural Economy" Rao, H.N., makes an attempt to evaluate and predict the role of banks in the rural economy. He opines that no doubt, commercial banks have contributed substantially for the development of rural sector mainly through agricultural development, but landless and small marginal farmers have not been benefited by the bank credit so far. He emphasises that the banks shall have to pay a leading role in this respect in the days to come[17].

In an article "Bank Lending-Thumb support for industrialisation of rural India", Batnagar, J.S., says that banks have played a significant role in the field of rural industrial progress. They are not merely lending agencies but also act as catalysts in the development process by providing credit for rural industries which provide gainful employment to the rural population[18].

In an article entitled "Regional Rural Banks – An Analysis", N.B. Shete makes an attempt to describe the need and evolution of RRBs. He also stressed the performance of RRBs by giving more details about purpose wise advances made by the RRBs and also explained the recovery position of RRBs[19].

Balishter's article "Performance of RRBs - An Evaluation" deals with the performance of RRBs in meeting agricultural needs of rural people. He also explained in his article about the evolution and growth of RRBs, deposit mobilisation of RRBs and recovery performance of RRBs[20].

Karthikeyan, A., in his article "Rural Development of Banks" has discussed the priority sector advances by banks for rural development. He opined that the credit expansion of these sectors did create an impact in agricultural production, development of small industries and employment generation through service and business sectors. He further feels that the development in rural areas is not in proportion to the quantum of finance deployed by the banks after the nationalisation because of these reasons: (i) wrong identification of borrowers; (ii) improper appraisal of the loan proposals and (iii) non-verification of end use[21].

In an article "Rural Credit Scenario in India" Ranga Rajan, C., the then Governor, Reserve Bank of India, at the silver Jubilee celebrations of the college of Agricultural Banking at Pune on January 12, 1995 highlighted the rural credit position. In his key note address regarding the rural banks, several factors have affected the operational efficiency and viability of RRBs such as high establishment and operational cost, low level of business, restricted area of operation and the like. Consequently, a number of RRBs have been showing negative results. During 1993, 173 RRBs had incurred losses out of 196. However, measures have been taken to enable the RRBs to diversify operations, relocating branches, increasing their non-target group lending from 40 per cent to 60 per cent[22].

Sankaraiah, T and Bhaghavan Reddy, B., in their article "Recovery performance of Rayalaseema Grameena Bank" made an attempt to study the trends in the recovery efficiency of the RGB. They concluded that the recovery drives adopted by the bank were defective. On the other hand, growing overdues reveal that the RGB has not maintained any balance between disbursement and recovery of loans[23].

Review note brought out by Culcutta Regional Office of NABARD, titled "Review of the working of the Regional Rural Banks", has provided the information about all India perspective of the RRBs and the performance of RRBs of West Bengal as on March 1987. It is observed that the annual losses of RRBs recorded a steep raise. A number of RRBs went for non-target group lending in a big way[24].

Uma Rani Das in her article captioned "performance and Prospects of RRBs" observed that the financial position of the

R.R.Bs has been in a very bad shape. Most of the RRBs are incurring losses and their operational efficiency is at the low level[25].

In an article "Do Rural Banks Matter? Evidence from the Indian Social Banking Experiment", authored by Rabin Bergers and Rohini Ponde, explained the key reasons, why poor people remain poor. They also explained that the impact of opening of rural banks on poverty and output. They suggested that Indian rural branch expansion programme significantly lowered rural poverty and increased non-agricultural output[26].

Butt, N. and Thoratt, Y., in their article "India's Regional Rural Banks: The Institutional Dimension of Reforms", stated the key success for reform process of Regional Rural Banks. He observed that political support for the reform process is a key determinant to the extent of which the Regional Rural Banks can be turned around. The reforms introduced since 1993 have not adequately addressed the incompatibility of the incentives, and provide recommendations for getting incentives right[27].

"Micro Finance Institutions (MFIs) in India", a seminar paper of Muralidhar Rao, K., General Manager, NABARD, Mumbai, at Manila on Regulation of MFIs, in July 2004, highlighted the emergence and position of MFIs in India. In his address on MFIs, he explained the range of institutions in public and private sector, offers micro finance service in India. According to him, there is at least one retail credit outlet for about 5000 rural people. In his paper an attempt is made to deal with various aspects relating to emergence of private micro finance industry in the extent of prevailing legal and regulatory environment for private sector rural and micro finance operators[28].

Sambi Reddy, B., in his article, "Assessment and Identification of Rural Poor in India: A study based on NSS household data", analysed and estimated the incidence of poverty in different sections of population using State-Specific poverty lines. The major states in India were classified into three poverty zones - High, Medium and Low poverty States on the basis of magnitude of the rural poverty ratios. In his paper, a new methodology was developed to identify the poor in rural areas. Index of deprivation was used to measure deprivation levels of individual households, which classify the households into poor, and non-poor[29].

In an article "Revisiting the lending infrastructure and changing the Mindset-Critical to Farm Lending", Yerramraju, B., explained the institutional credit for agriculture and allied activities. He analysed the debt profile of rural households. He also mentioned the role of NABARD in shaping the investment credit in agriculture and measures that can strengthen the system of agricultural credit[30].

Sharma, R.D and Gurjeet., in their article "Strategy for Customer Satisfaction in Rural Banks-A Case Study of Shivalik Kshetriya Gramin Bank, Hoshiyapur" stated the nature and extent of customer satisfaction in regional rural banks through customer opinion and works out a strategic action plan. Shivalik Kshetriya Gramina bank, Hoshiyapur in Punjab was selected to workout the level of customer satisfaction in this bank by using Likert's 5 points scale[31].

In an article "Productivity Growth in Regional Rural Banks", Amarender Reddy, A., examines total factor productivity, technical and scale efficiency changes in regional rural banks by using the data from 192 banks for the period 1996 to 2002. He further says that rural banks showed significant economies of scale in terms of assets and number of branches under each bank. Banks located in economically developed areas have exhibited significantly higher productivity growth[32].

Sarma, R.H., in his article, "Will RRB mergers lead to efficient rural lending?" pointed out that amalgamations of RRBs would not automatically improve efficiency but would enlarge their area of operation and business opportunities. He also mentioned that low credit-deposit ratio is a cause for low profitability. Because of lazy banking tendencies in rural banks, people deposit their surpluses with the sponsor banks. He clearly opined that there should be a change in the mindset of the employees and the management[33].

NEED FOR THE STUDY

It is evident from the review of literature that rural development as an area of research continues to fascinate the social science researchers. A large number of the poorest of the poor continued to remain outside the fold of the formal banking system. These studies also showed that the existing banking policies, systems and procedures, and deposit and loan procedures were perhaps not well suited to meet the most immediate needs of the poor. Any study made with regard to RRBs and rural development in a particular area may not be relevant to other areas as India is a vast country with different socio-economic conditions. Further, the reforms in banking sector had made the earlier studies irrelevant to the present situation prevailing. Therefore, there is a dire need to undertake area specific studies. The present study, therefore, is an endeavour to examine the role of RRBs in rural development in a socially and economically backward area of the state of Andhra Pradesh i.e., Cuddapah district of Rayalseema.

OBJECTIVES OF THE STUDY

The study specifically aims at:

- reviewing the progress made by the RRBs in India;
- evaluating the performance of Rayalaseema Grameena Bank [RGB] Cuddapah;
- assessing the impact of RGB financing on Rural Development; and
- identifying the problems of the beneficiaries vis-à-vis bank officials.

HYPOTHESIS

The present study pre-supposes that there is no significant rural development in Cuddapah district of Andhra Pradesh through the credit deployed by Rayaseema Grameena Bank, Cuddapah. The hypothesis would be tested with the help of different characteristic variables of rural development.

SAMPLE DESIGN

Rayalaseema Grameena Bank sponsored by Syndicate Bank was established on 6th August 1976, under the RRBs Act 1976 with its Head Quarters at Cuddapah. The RGB's operational area covers three districts of Andhra Pradesh viz., Cuddapah, kurnool and Markapur Division of Prakasam. The RGB has 148 branches covering all three districts. For the purpose of selection of sample, the multi-stage and simple random techniques have been adopted.

Table 1
Description of the Sample Size

Service Areas of RGB, Cuddapah	*Rural Branches*	*Select Branches*	*Universe of Beneficiaries of Select Branches*	*Sample Beneficiaries*
Cuddapah	12	1	1407	141
Proddatur	18	2	3978	398
Rajampet	19	2	1350	135
Total	49	5	6735	674

Source : Official records of RGB, Cuddapah.

In the first stage, the area of the study has been narrowed down purposively to Cuddapah district only. The RGB has 49 rural branches, 10 semi urban branches and five urban branches, in its three service areas (Cuddapah, Proddatur, and Rajempet) of Cuddapah district. Since the present study is confined to rural development, the rural branches are only considered for the purpose of study in the second stage. Hence, the universe of the study constitutes 49 rural branches covering three service areas of RGB viz., Cuddapah [12], Proddatur [18] and Rajampet [19]. In the third stage, 10 per cent of the total rural branches has been selected at random. The sample, thus, constitutes five rural branches consisting of 6,735 beneficiaries. These beneficiaries spread over three service areas namely, Cuddapah [1407], Proddatur [3978] and Rajampet [1350]. In the final stage, 10 per cent of beneficiaries from select branches representing 674 beneficiaries-141 beneficiaries from Cuddapah, 398 from Proddatur and 135 from Rajampet Service areas-has been chosen at random. The sample beneficiaries are involved in different economic activities, such as agriculture and allied activities, small business, rural artisans, milk trade and also daily wage earning through hard labour. They also represent different social and economic strata of the population of the study area.

PERIOD OF THE STUDY

For the purpose of evaluating the performance of RGB, a moderate study period of six years commencing from 1998 - 1999 and ending with 2003 -2004 has been adopted. To asses the impact of RGB financing on the socio-economic status of the beneficiaries, one year period starting with April 2002 and ending with March 2003, has been considered.

SCOPE OF THE STUDY

The present study is a microlevel and area specific study. The scope of the study is confined to the objectives of the study as specified earlier. The present study is limited to the rural branches of RGB operating in Cuddapah district only.

DATA BASE

The data and information for the present study have been obtained from primary and secondary sources. The primary information has been gathered from the sample beneficiaries and bank officials by administering structured schedules designed for the purpose. The secondary data have been collected from the published and unpublished reports of the Reserve Bank of India, Bombay; National Bank for Agricultural and Rural Development [NABARD] Bombay; National Institute of Rural Development, Hyderabad; Annual Reports; District Credit plans, Annual Action plans, and other publications of RGB, Cuddapah. Journals and magazines concerning Banking, Finance and Rural Development were also referred to.

TOOLS OF ANALYSIS

The data collected from different quarters are analyzed with the help of statistical tools and techniques such as percentages, averages, ratios, variance of analysis, students' 't' test, chi-square test and other statistical tests for drawing meaningfull conclusions.

CHAPTERISATION

The thesis is organized into *Seven* Chapters

Chapter-1	:	Introduction
Chapter-2	:	Regional Rural Banks: An Overview
Chapter-3	:	Research Design and Methodology
Chapter-4	:	Performance Evaluation of RGB
Chapter-5	:	Impact of RGB Financing on Rural Development
Chapter-6	:	Problems of the Beneficiaries vis-a vis Bank Officials
Chapter-7	:	Summary, Conclusions and Suggestions

REFERENCES

1. Ghosal, S.N. (1972), *Agricultural Financing in India,* New Delhi: Asia Publishing House.
2. Charan D. (1980), *Wadhwa Rural Banking for Rural Development,* Delhi: MacMillan Company.
3. Pany, R.K. (1985), *Institutional Credit for Agricultural in India,* New Delhi: Ashish Publishing House.
4. Naidu, L.K., (edited) (1988), *Bank Finance for Rural Development,* Seminar paper on Commercial Banks in Chittoor District, New Delhi: Ashish Publishing House.
5. Narayan,N and Chandrasekhar, G. (1988), *Bank Credit and Rural Development–A Study of Utilisation of Credit in Anatapur District,* New Delhi: Ashish Publishing House.
6. Sunil Kumar (1990), *Regional Rural Bank and Rurl Development,* New Delhi: Deep and Deep Publications.
7. Bala Mohan Das, V., Prabhakar Rao., J.V. Hrushikesava Rao,P. (1991), *Rural Banks and Rural Credit* Discovery, Publishing House.
8. Krishnamaraju, S. (1992), *Banking Finance and Rural Development,* New Delhi: Discovery Publishing House.

9. Patnaik, U.C. and Mishra, R.N (1993), *Rural Banking in India*, New Delhi: Anmol Publications Pvt., Ltd.
10. Priyan, A.K. (1995), *Regional Rural Banks Rural Development*, Jaipur: Arihant Publishing House.
11. Sandhu, B.S. (1996), *Banking and Rural Development*, New Delhi: Deep and Deep Publications.
12. Archana Singhal, B.S. Yadhav (2005), *Role of Regional Banks in Rural Development*, New Delhi: Sree Publishers and Distributers.
13. Pati, A.P. (2005), *Regional Rural Banks in Liberelised Environment*, New Delhi: Mittal Publications.
14. Acharya Shyama Charan & Mohanty, Ashok Kumar (2006), *Operational Analysis-Regional Rural Banks*, Delhi: Soujanya Books.
15. Khemani, C.L. and Balakrishanan, K.V. (1983), *Financing Weaker Sections: Importance of Consumption Credit*, Agricultural Banking, Some Operational Aspects.
16. Mishra, M.N. (1987), *Rural Banking for Rural Poor, Yojana*, Vol.34, No.IV, April.
17. Rao, H.N. (1987), *Exapinding Role of Banks in Rural Economy, The Banker*, Publication Division, Govt of India, Vol.34, No.9, November.
18. Batnagar, J.S. (1987), *Banks Lending thumb support for Industrialization of Rural India, Agriculture Banker*, Vol.9, No.1, Jan-March.
19. Shete, N.B. (1990), *Regional Rural Banks-An Analysis, Banking Finance*, Vol.3, No.4, April.
20. Balister (1991), *Performance of Regional Rural Banks-An Evaluation, Banking Finance*, Vol.4, No.5, May.
21. Karthikeyan, A. (1994), *Rural Developments by Banks, Banking Finance*,Vol.8, No.7, July.
22. Rangarajan, C. (1995), *Rural Credit Scenario in India*, An Address of Silver Jublee Selebrations of Collage of Agricultural Banking at Pune, Jan.12.
23. Sankaraiah, T. and Bhagavan Reddy, B. (1998), *Recovery Performance of Rayalaseema Grameena Bank, Banking Finance*, Vol.XI, No. 11, November.
24. Review Note Brought out by Culcutta Regional Office of NABARD, Review of the Working of the Regional Rural Banks, *Banking Finance*, Vol. XI, No.11, Nov.98.

25. Umarani Das (1998), *Perfomance and Prospects of R.R.Bs, Banking Finance,* Vol.XI, No.11, November.

26. Robin Burggess & Rohini Ponde (2003), *Do Rural Banks Matter? Evidence from the Indian Social Banking Experiment,* Suntory and Toyota International centers for Economics and Related Disciplines, LSE in its Series STICERD-Development Economics Papers, No.40, August.

27. Butt, N and Thorat,Y. (2004), "Indias's Regional Rural Banks: The Institutional Dimension of Reforms", *National Bank News* Review, NBARD, Vol.20, No.2&3, April-September.

28. Muralidhar Rao, K. (2004), *Micro Finance Institutions in India,* Seminar Paper presented at Manila on Regulation of mFIs in July.

29. Sambi Reddy, B. (2004), *Assessment and Identification of Rural Poor in India: A Study based on NSS Households Data, National Bank News Review, NBARD,* Vol. 20, No.2&3, April-September.

30. Yerramraju, B. (2004), *Revisiting the Lending Infrastructure and Changing the Mindset-Critical to Farm Lending, National Bank News Review, NBARD,* Vol. 20, No.2&3, April-September.

31. Sharm, R.D and Gurgeet Kaur (2004), *Strategy for Customer Satisfaction in Rural Banks–A Case Study of Shivalik Kshetrya Gramin Bank, Hoshiapur, National Bank News Review, NBARD,* Vol. 20, No.2&3, April-September.

32. Amarender Reddy (2006), *Productivity Growth in Regional Rural Banks, Economic and Political Weekly,* March 18, (1079)

33. Sarma, R.H., *Will RRB Mergers Lead to Efficient Rural Banking? Business Line,* September 23, 2005.

4

Performance Evaluation of RGB

Among the various infrastructural facilities for economic development and eradication of poverty, providing adequate banking facilities is very important. Availability of credit facilities is an essential condition for the socio-economic development of the poor whether living in urban or rural areas. In this context, RRBs have emanated as right institutions to extend credit facilities to the weaker sections of the population. RRBs have proved themselves as a superior form of financing institutions for the weaker sections of the population over the co-operatives and the commercial banks. The present Chapter tries to evaluate the performance of "Rayalaseema Grameena Bank", Cuddapah.

Rayalaseema Grameena Bank (RGB) was established on 6th August 1976 with its Headquarters at Cuddapah in the state of Andhra Pradesh, under the RRBs Act 1976. RGB is one among the 10 RRBs sponsored by the Syndicate Bank. The area of operation of the Bank covers three districts - entire Cuddapah and Kurnool districts and Markapur Revenue Division of Prakasam district. The bank has been playing pivotal role in economic development of its area of operation and continued to be a pioneer in extending credit to priority sector. The year 2001-02 was a land mark in the history of the bank as the Bank completed 25 years of its purposeful existence. The Bank has occupied the "Number one" Position amongst the 16 RRBs in the state. The bank is ranked at '4' out of 196 RRBs at national level in a dynamic weighted ranking of RRBs. This exercise was conducted by the "Financial Express"[1].

OBJECTIVES OF RAYALASEEMA GRAMEENA BANK

RGB was established with the following objectives:

- to extend credit facilities to the weaker and neglected sectors of the society with special reference to Integrated Rural Development Programme (IRDP), and District Rural Industries Project (DRIP) on a pilot basis in Kurnool district in Southern India;
- to ensure integrated support to rural industrialisation for increased production and income earning opportunities through setting-up of non-farm units in the rural areas on a commercially viable basis;
- to provide banking facilities in remote and unbanked areas; and
- to inculcate banking habits among the rural masses so as to tap idle money through mobilization of deposits and to lend it for productive purposes.

ORGANISATIONAL ASPECTS

RGB is controlled by the Board of Directors comprising of nine members, including the Chairman. Three members of the Board of Directors are nominated by the Central Government (in addition to Chairman), two by the State Government, and three by the sponsored bank.

Cadre-wise Staff Position

The recruitment of the staff of the bank is made by the Board of Directors on the basis of written test followed by oral examination. The minimum qualification is bachelor degree for the manager and officer; matriculation for clerk-cum-cashiers. The cadre-wise staff position is presented in Table 1.

It is obvious that the total strength of the staff is 942. Of these, Scale III officers are 21 spreading seven each in Head Office, Area offices and Branches respectively. About 118 are working in the cadre of Scale II Officers, spreading 11 in Head Office, five in Area Offices and 102 in all the branches. There are 212 Scale I Officers. Of these, about 16 working in Head Office, six in Area Offices and 190 are working in Branch Offices. Totally, there are 433 clerk cum cashiers, 158 Messengers including drivers, working in the own spectrum of RGB.

Table 1
Cadre-wise Staff Position of RGB as on 31st March 2004

Cadre	*Head Office*	*Area Offices*	*Branches*	*Total*
Scale III Officers	7	7	7	21
Scale II Officers	11	5	102	118
Scale I Officers	16	6	190	212
Clerk- cum-cashiers	25	12	396	433
Messengers/drivers	7	6	145	158
Total	66	36	840	942

Sourse: Annual Report of RGB, Cuddapah, 2003-04

Branch Net Work

RGB has spread its operations to three districts such as Cuddapah, Kurnool and Markapur division of Prakasm district. The district-wise break up of branches is shown in Table 2. It is evident that the RGB has 148 branches covering all the three districts. There exist 107 rural branches, 30 semi urban branches and 11 urban branches. District-wise particulars show that it has 69 branches in Cuddapah district, 64 branches in Kurnool district and 15 branches in Prakasam

Table 2
Branch Network of RGB as on March 2004

District	*No.of Branches*	*Rural*	*Semi-urban*	*Urban*	*Extension Counters*	*Area Offices*	*FSCs*
Cuddapah	69	54	10	5	2	3	4
Kurnool	64	43	15	6	2	3	4
Prakasam	15	10	5	-	-	1	-
Total	148	107	30	11	4	7	8

Source: Annual Report of RGB, Cuddapah, 2003-04

district. Besides, the Bank has seven Area offices spreading three each in Cuddapah and Kurnool districts and one in Prakasam district. The Bank has also sponsored eight Farmer Services Cooperative Societies (FSCS), four each in Cuddapah and Kurnool districts.

FINANCIAL ASPECTS

Share Capital

The authorised capital of the bank was Rs. 5 crores[2]. Table 3 gives the data concerning the share capital position of RGB, Cuddapah.

Table 3
Share Capital of RGB as on March 2004

(Rs in lakhs)

Contributors	*Share Capital*	*Share Capital Deposit*
Central Government	50.00	737.56
Sponsor bank (Syndicate Bank)	35.00	516.29
Government of Andhra Pradesh	15.00	221.26
Total	100.00	1475.11

Source: Annual Reports of RGB,2003-2004.

The paid up capital of the Bank is Rs. 100 lakhs, contributed by Government of India, Sponsor Bank (Syndicate Bank) and Andhra Pradesh State Government in the ratio of 50:35:15 respectively. As a part of restructuring process, an additional share capital of Rs.1,475.11 lakhs was infused by the shareholders. Out of which Rs.737.56 lakhs by Central Government, Rs.516.29 lakhs by Syndicate Bank and Rs.221.26 lakhs was contributed by Andhra Pradesh State Government.

Deposits

Deposit is an important element determining the development of the bank. It depends upon the saving capacity of the areas in which the bank is operating. Deposits are the reserves of the people with the bank[3]. RGB had introduced demand deposits and various kinds of time deposits such as Janakalpa deposits,

Karshakamitra deposits, Samraksha deposits, Janabadbrata cash certificates, Iswarya cash certificates, Lakshmi cash certificates, Kamadenu deposits, Soubhagya deposits, Senior citizen deposits and the like to attract the rural mass.

Table 4 manifests the position of deposit mobilisation by the RGB. Number of Accounts and average deposits per branch are also embodied. It is obvious that the RGB could mobilize Rs.83,325.58 lakhs of deposits by the end of the year 2003-04 as against Rs.30,246.85 lakhs in 1998-99. The average deposit per branch has advanced from Rs.21.61 lakhs in 1998-99 to Rs.56.30 lakhs in 2003-04. A considerable progress is observed in deposits and average deposits per branch. The target of deposit mobilisation during the year was Rs.87,000 lakhs[3]. The RGB could achieve 95.78 per cent of the target. It may be inferred that the bank has performed well in respect of deposit mobilisation. The reason might be the introduction of attractive deposit schemes with attractive interest rates suitable to the rural areas. Further, RGB facilitates withdrawing the deposited money up to 90 per cent as and when the depositor requires.

Table 4
Deposits and Average Deposit Per Branch of RGB

(Rs in lakhs)

Year	*Deposits*	*No.of Branches*	*Average Deposit per Branch*
1998-99	30246.85 (692586)	140	21.61
1999-2k	36787.99 (722965)	140	26.28
2000-01	45947.93 (764435)	145	31.69
2001-02	57914.98 (791361)	148	39.13
2002-03	67002.69 (821113)	148	45.30
2003-04	83325.58 (855972)	148	56.30

Note: Figures in the parentheses indicate number of accounts
Source: Annual Reports of RGB, Cuddapah

Composition of Deposits

The total deposits of the bank are broadly classified into two categories such as Demand deposits and Term deposits. Demand deposits consist of current account deposits and savings deposits. Demand deposits can be withdrawn whenever the depositor needs while the Term deposits after a fixed period of time only. Table 5 presents the broad classification of deposits. It is evident that the proportion of Term deposits was higher when compared to the demand deposits. It constitutes more than 60 per cent to total deposits during all the years under study. Savings deposit stood at second place in terms of amount. Current and other deposits had occupied third place.

It is, further, observed that the percentage of term deposits declined from 72.64 in 1998-99 to 62.07 in 2003-04, though there was an upward trend in the year 1999-2k to 2001-02. Conversely, the percentage of saving deposits had showed a decline upto the year 2001-02 and thereafter depicted a rise. The reason is that the bank had concentrated more on improving of savings deposits of the bank by launching different savings schemes. The current deposits had phenomenally increased in absolute values from Rs. 833.14 lakhs in 1998-99, to Rs. 3446.35 lakhs in 2003-04.

The coefficient of correlation is calculated to know the relationship between demand deposits and term deposits. The results show that the 'r' between these two variables is -0.197. It means that there exists marginal negative relationship between demand deposits and term deposits of RGB in different years under study.

Outstanding Advances

The banking institutions are the custodians of private savings and powerful instruments to provide credit. They mobilize the resources of the country by accepting deposits and chanalise them for industrial and national development by granting loans[4]. The objective of the RGB is to bring a change in the socio-economic conditions of the weaker sections of the society. Keeping this objective in view, the bank had drafted credit plans by assessing the credit requirements of each village in the service area of each branch. Adequate credit limits are granted to the branches under various sections depending on the overdue position to ensure timely flow of credit to the needy clientele.

Table 5

Statement Showing Composition of Deposits of RGB

(Rs.in lakhs)

Years	Demand Deposits							
	Current other Accounts		Saving Deposits		Term Deposits		Total	
	No.of Accounts	Amount	No.of Accounts	Amount	No.of Accounts	Amount	No.of Accounts	Amount
1998-99	49689	833.14 (2.75)	482324	7443.39 (24.61)	160573	21970.32 (72.64)	692586	30246.85 (100)
1999-2k	54402	930.11 (2.53)	489137	8048.97 (21.88)	179426	27808.91 (75.59)	722965	36787.99 (100)
2000-01	67020	1042.32 (2.27)	496303	9701.36 (21.11)	201112	35204.25 (76.62)	764435	45947.93 (100)
2001-02	45712	1460.80 (2.52)	528444	12960.71 (22.38)	217205	43493.47 (75.10)	791361	57914.98 (100)
2002-03	46376	2175.91 (3.25)	567713	17600.51 (26.27)	207024	472262.27 (70.48)	821113	6700269 (100)
2003-04	N.A	3446.35 (4.14)	N.A	28159.02 (33.79)	200217	51720.21 (62.07)	855972	83325.58 (100)

Note: Figures in the parentheses represent percentage to total

Source: Annual Reports of RGB, Cuddapah

The bank has been providing not only the agriculture loans, but also non-agricultural loans to the poor people like loans to rural artisans, transport operators, retail trade, Self Help Groups (SHGs) and the like. Besides, the bank has launched various schemes under Integrated Rural Development Programme (IRDP), Scheduled Caste Action Plan (SCAP), and Scheduled Tribe Action Plan (STAP) in order to drive out the regional imbalances and also to improve the living conditions of the rural poor.

The bank also conducts credit camps in order to provide financial assistance to the poor and needy persons. The main purpose of organising credit camps is to cover the maximum beneficiaries by providing them all kinds of financial assistance within a short span of time. Further, the National Bank for Agriculture and Rural Development (NABARD) has identified the rural non-farm sector as a "Thrust Area". It has made efforts for growth and development of the sector as a means for employment generation and income augmentation to the rural population. Keeping this objective, NABARD has launched "District Rural Industries Project" (DRIP) on a pilot basis in Kurnool district in southern India to ensure integrated support to rural industrialisation for increased production and income earning opportunities setting-up of non-farm units in rural areas on a commercially viable basis.

Table 6
Statement Showing Outstanding Advances and Average Advance Per Branch of RGB

(Rs in lakhs)

Year	*Outstanding Advances*	*No.of Branches*	*Average Advance per Branch*
1998-1999	24163.14 (234580)	140	172.59
1999-2000	26308.81 (220566)	140	187.92
2000-2001	31344.86 (232119)	145	216.17
2001-2002	37992.58 (242350)	148	256.72
2002-2003	45118.30 (246901)	148	304.85
2003-2004	56942.30 (263062)	148	384.75

Note: Figures in the parentheses indicate number of accounts
Source: Annual Reports of RGB, Cuddapah

Table 6 displays outstanding advances and average advances per branches of RGB, Cuddapah during 1999-2004. It is clear that the total amount of outstanding advances was Rs.24,163.14 lakhs in 1998-99 and it augmented to Rs.56,942.36 lakhs in 2003-04. But the improvement in number of accounts was low as the RGB could open a limited number of branches, during the period of five years under study.

When viewed from average advances per branch, it had augmented from Rs.172.59 lakhs in 1998-99 to Rs.384.75 lakhs in 2003-04. It is evident that an improvement in outstanding advances is found over the years. This trend is in tune with the objectives of RGB and shows the determination of RGB to serve the weaker and neglected sections of the society. Despite this, the bank has to bridge the gap between demand and supply of credit in rural areas.

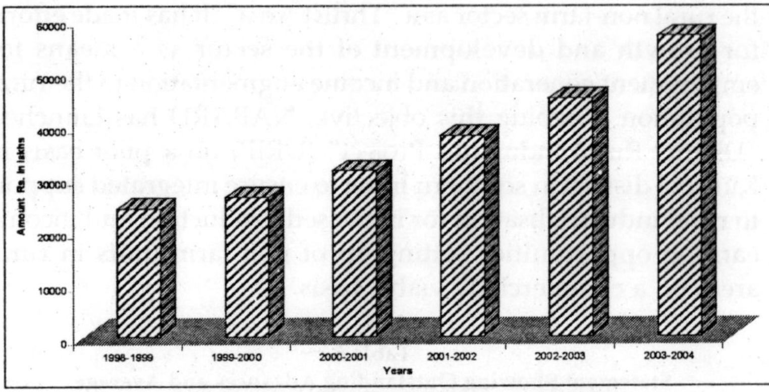

Figure 1: Outstanding Advances of RGB

Credit Deposit Ratio

Credit Deposit ratio is core element to determine the growth of the bank. A favorable increasing Credit Deposit ratio of the bank is of significance in order to meet the credit requirements of the rural areas and to push up the rate of growth in the rural areas. Rural areas cannot be neglected for longer period as it will depress the process of growth in the urban areas and thereby, overall economic growth. A higher and increasing credit-deposit ratio is desirable. Table 7 depicts the Credit Deposit ratio of the RGB.

Table 7
Credit Deposit Ratio of RGB, Cuddapah

(Rs. in Lakhs)

Year	*Deposits*	*Advances*	*C/D Ratio*
1998-99	30246.85	24163.14	79.88
1999-2k	36787.99	26308.81	71.51
2000-01	45947.93	31344.86	68.22
2001-02	57914.98	37992.58	65.80
2002-03	67002.69	45118.30	67.33
2003-04	83325.58	56942.30	68.30

Source: Annual Reports of RGB, Cuddapah

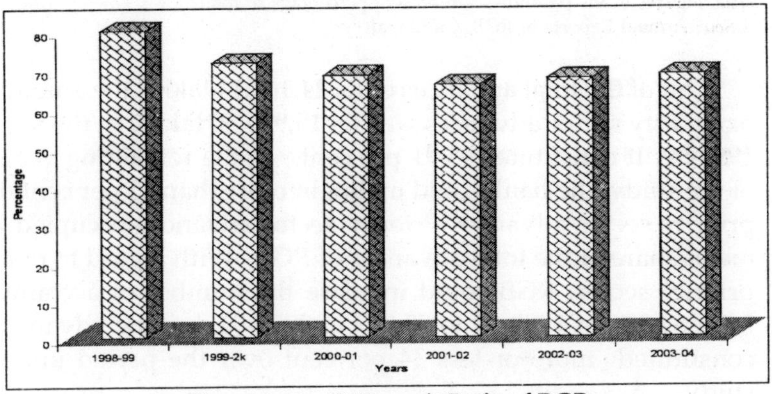

Figure 2: Credit Deposit Ratio of RGB

It is evident that the Credit Deposit ratio had slumped down from 79.88 per cent in 1998-99 to 68.30 per cent in the concluding year i.e., 2003-04, with mild fluctuations during the period under study. Though the deposits and advances have been increasing continuously, the declining credit deposit ratio could be observed upto 2001-02. It means that the rate of increase in advances was low in relation to deposits. It may be inferred that a declining credit deposit ratio indicates that the RGB could not lend the mobilized resources from local areas for the benefit of the weaker sections of the society in the right perspective.

Sector-Wise Classification of Advances

Sector-wise classification of outstanding advances of RGB is shown in Table 8.

Table 8
Sector-wise Classification of Outstanding Advances of RGB

(Rs in lakhs)

	Priority Sector		*Non-priority Sector*		
Year	*No.of Accounts*	*Amount*	*No.of Accounts*	*Amount*	*Total*
1998-99	152246	15925.50 (65.91)	82334	8237.64 (34.09)	24163.14 (100)
1999-2k	145662	17731.15 (67.40)	85979	8577.66 (32.60)	26308.81 (100)
2000-01	148851	20749.25 (66.20)	83260	10595.61(33.80)	31344.86 (100)
2001-02	149371	24860.02 (65.44)	92979	13132.56(34.56)	37992.58 (100)
2002-03	155346	29848.24 (66.16)	91555	15270.06 (33.84)	45118.30 (100)
2003-04	170765	37468.45 (65.81)	92297	19473.85(34.19)	56942.30 (100)

Note: Figures in the parentheses represent percentage to total
Source: Annual Reports of RGB, Cuddapah

Out of the total advances of Rs 24,163.14 lakhs, the amount of priority sector advances was Rs 15,925.50 lakhs, in the year 1998-99. It constitutes 65.91 per cent. In the remaining years of the study, the bank could maintain more than 65 per cent of priority sector advances Priority sector advances occupied a major share of the total advances of RGB. With regard to non-priority sector, RGB could increase the number of accounts from 82,334 in 1998-99 to 92,297 in 2003-04, but the advances constituted more or less 34 per cent over the period under study.

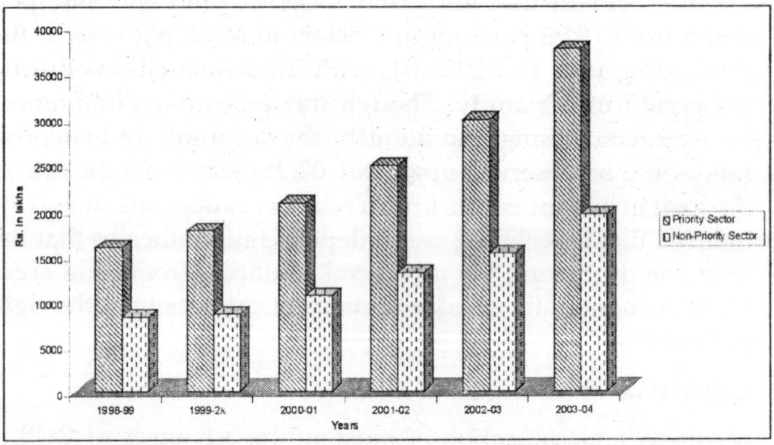

Figure 3: Priority and Non-Priority Sector Advances of RGB

To examine the variances between the priority sector and non-priority sector advances, student's 't' test has been applied. As per the results, ' t ' calculated value is 6.72 and Table value is for 5 degrees of freedom at 5% level of significance is 2.57. It is evident that 't' calculated value is higher than Table value and thereby indicating that there is a significant difference between priority sector and non-priority sector outstanding advances by RGB. To be precise, the formulated hypothesis that there is no significant difference between the means of these variables is rejected.

Classification of Priority sector Advances

Distribution of credit among different categories of priority sector borrowers of RGB is shown in Table 9. It is apparent that the agriculture credit though increased to 86 per cent in 1999-2000, had declined considerably to 75.83 per cent in 2003-04. RGB has allocated major chunk of funds to agriculture purpose out of the total credit. Retail trade could occupy second place in receiving the loans from the RGB. The percentage of credit to retail trade has reported an upward trend from 7.42 in 1998-99 to 8.22 in 2003-04 except in the year 1999-2000. The percentage of credit to small scale industries and rural artisans decreased from 2.93 in 1998-99 to 1.10 in 2003-04. The same trend can be observed in the transport operators also. It decreased abnormally from 3.51 per cent in 1998-99 to 0.69 in 2003-04. A steady growth in the percentage of SHGs was registered. It was 0.20 per cent in 1999-2000 and increased to 5.87 per cent in 2003-04. The other advances were fluctuating between three per cent and five per cent during the period under study with the exception of 2003-04. It is inferred that the bank has given priority to agriculture and agriculture-allied activities while sanctioning the loans. But the percentage of credit had declined. The reason is that the mounting overdues in these activities are very high. The same situation is also observed in small scale industries, rural artisans and transport operators. In the case of SHGs, advances had depicted a rise as Government is evincing keen importance to sanction the loans to these groups.

Table 9
Classification of Priority Sector Advances by RGB

(Rs.in lakhs)

Year	Agriculture		Small-scale Industries/rural Artisans		Retail Trade	
	No.of Accounts	Amount	No.of Accounts	Amount	No.of Accounts	Amount
1998-99	114600	13071.71 (82.08)	8808	467.40 (2.93)	18357	1181.77(7.42)
1999-2k	114067	15249.12 (86.00)	7131	388.27 (2.19)	15941	1100.68(6.20)
2000-01	116337	17326.31 (83.50)	6040	360.05 (1.74)	19647	1638.35 (7.90)
2001-02	117650	20583.80 (82.80)	5187	363.45 (1.46)	19129	1955.12(7.86)
2002-03	122303	24464.02 (81.96)	3953	352.91 (1.18)	19702	2431.67(8.15)
2003-04	131051	28414.12 (75.83)	3446	412.44 (1.10)	21522	3079.39(8.22)

Contd.

Transport Operators		Self -Help Groups		Others		Total
No.of Accounts	Amount	No.of Accounts	Amount	No.of Accounts	Amount	
931	558.59 (3.51)	–	–	9550	646.07 (4.06)	15925.50(100)
694	409.46 (2.31)	209	35.50 (0.20)	7620	548.12 (3.09)	17731.15(100)
645	373.66 (1.80)	1974	271.59 (1.31)	3816	779.29 (3.75)	20749.25(100)
474	295.21 (1.19)	3508	595.56 (2.40)	3423	1066.88(4.29)	24860.02(100)
377	286.00 (0.96)	5457	1036.11(3.47)	3554	1277.53(4.28)	29848.24(100)
420	259.25 (0.69)	9845	2198.08(5.87)	4481	3105.17(8.29)	37468.45(100)

Note: Figures in the parentheses indicate percentage to total
Source: Annual reports of RGB, Cuddapah

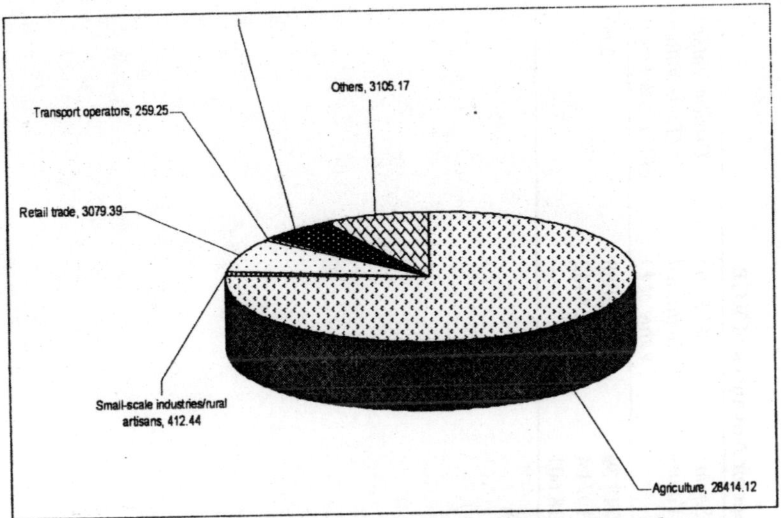

Figure 4: Classification of Priority Sector Outstanding Advances by RGB for the year 2003-2004

With a view to testing the significance of variations in between the segments of priority sector advances and various years under study, the 'F' test (Analysis of Variance) has been applied.

Table 10 portrays that the calculated value of 'F' ratio for different years is 2.2. The Table value of 'F' at 5% level of significance for V1 = 5 and V2 = 25, is 2.6. It is obvious that 'F' calculated value is grater than the Table value. Hence, it is concluded that there is significant difference between the years pertaining to priority sector advances by RGB.

The calculated value of 'F' ratio in between the different segments of the priority sector advances is 2.208. The Table value of 'F' at 5% level of significance for V1=5 and V2=25 is 2.6. It indicates that 'F' calculated value is less than the Table value at 5% level of significance. It is quite apparent that there exists no significant difference between various segments of priority sector advances by RGB in Cuddapah District.

Table 11 displays the outstanding advances for the agricultural and non-agricultural sectors. It is apparent that loans and advances outstanding in farm sector was Rs 13071.67

Table 10
Analysis of Variance in Classification of Priority Sector Advances of RGB

Source of Variance	*Sum of Squares*	*Degree of Freedom*	*Mean Square Values*	*'F' Ratio (Caluculated Value of F)*	*Critical Values (Table Values of F at 5% Level)*
Segments of priority sector	55048741.96	V1=5	11009748.39	2.2088	2.60
Between Years	1803005537	V1=5	3606011074.4	72.3442	
Error or Residual	124612965.0	V2=25	4984518.601	–	

Source: Computed on the basis of data furnished in Table 5.9

lakhs in 1998-99. It constitutes 54.10 per cent in total advances. This proportion was continued with minor fluctuations upto 2002-03.

But in the year 2003-04, it was reduced to 49.90 per cent. Conversely, outstanding advances to non-farm sector increased slightly, which registered 50.10 per cent in 2003-04. It is obvious that the percentage of loans to agriculture started to decrease while the coverage of non-agriculture sector increased. The reason might be the poor recovery performance in agriculture loans.

Coefficient of correlation has been calculated to asses the relationship between the agricultural and non-agricultural loans. The coefficient of correlation between these two variables is 0.98. It signifies that there exists a very high positive relation between the agricultural and non-agricultural loans.

Programme-Wise Advances by RGB

The programme-wise advances include Swarna Jayanthi Gram Swarajgar Yojana [SGSY), Scheduled Caste Action Plan (SCAP)/Scheduled Tribe Action Plan (STAP), Back Ward Caste Action Plan (BCAP) and Others. These programmes are undertaken to drive out the poverty of rural masses and effective rural development.

Programme-wise advances given by RGB are embodied in Table 12. It is evident that the total units grounded under different programmes in 1999-2k were 1,641. Out of this, units under IRDP/SGSY were 1,337. The total amount disbursed to all the programmes was Rs. 109.71 lakhs. The share of IRDP/ SGSY was Rs. 80.55 lakhs (73.42 per cent). The disbursement of loans had reached to Rs. 164.01 lakhs in 2003-04 under this programme. But the number of units grounded had come down to 311. It is observed that RGB put more efforts to ground the more number of units in the initial years later on, it reduced the grounding of the units and increased the amount of finance.

It means that loan amount to each unit has increased. With regard to SCAP/STAP, RGB launched 157 units in 1999-2k with uneven fluctuations it reached to 232 units in 2003-04. The

Table 11
Agriculture and Non-agriculture Advances of RGB, Cuddapah

(Rs.in lakhs)

Year	Agriculture Activities		Non-Agriculture Activities		Total Amount
	No.of Accounts	Amount	No.of Accounts	Amount	
1998-99	114600	13071.67 (54.10)	119980	11091.47 (45.90)	24163.14 (100)
1999-2k	113808	14715.61 (55.93)	106758	11593.20 (44.07)	26308.81 (100)
2000-01	116737	17326.31 (55.28)	115382	14018.55 (44.72)	31344.86 (100)
2001-02	117650	20583.80 (54.18)	124700	17408.78 (45.82)	37992.58 (100)
2002-03	122303	24464.02 (54.22)	124598	20654.28 (45.78)	45118.30 (100)
2003-04	131051	28414.12 (49.90)	132011	28528.18 (50.10)	56942.30 (100)

Note: Figures in the parentheses indicate percentage to total
Source: Annual Reports of RGB, Cuddapah.

amount of loan provided under this plan was Rs. 36.09 lakhs in the year 2003-2004. In case of BCAP, RGB had grounded 57 units in 1999-2k and the number of units registered as 31 in 2003-04. Loans disbursed to these units were fluctuated between Rs 5.19 lakhs and Rs. 6.42 lakhs during the study period. Similarly loans to other programmes also had varied in between 7.15 per cent and 22.14 per cent over the period of study. It is inferred that the RGB did not follow any procedure to fix the targets per year regarding the grounding of units under any programme. Based on the viability of the project only, it sanctions the loan. It is further observed that RGB has given more priority to SGSY when compared to other programmes.

Micro Finance

Financing of Self-Help Groups (SHGs) is one of the thrust areas. Loans provided by banks to SHGs will be reckoned as priority sector lending[5] .The bank has made continued consistent efforts in forming/promotion of SHGs and linkage of these Groups by providing credit. Women Development Cell at Head office of the bank had closely associated and monitored the branches in implementation of this Micro-Credit Programme.

Table 13 shows the statement concerning the SHG linkages, loans disbursed and loans outstanding under SHGs. It is evident that about 275 SHGs were linked and Rs. 52.89 lakhs was released to the groups during 1999-2k. Loan amount outstanding was Rs. 35.50 lakhs in 1999-2k. In the year 2003-04, about 7,753 groups were linked and an amount of Rs.2,099.93 lakhs was disbursed. The credit outstanding at the end of 2003-04 was Rs.2,198.08 lakhs. It is apparent that SHG linkage had spurt over the years. Consequently, loan amount disbursed by RGB had reported a rise over the years under reference. It can be said that the RGB has been evincing keen interest towards the SHGs. Undoubtedly, this trend is paving the way for rural development by the RGB.

Table 12

Govt Sponsored Programme-wise Disbursements of Loans by RGB, Cuddapah

(Rs. in Lakhs)

Year	*IRDP/SGSY*		*SCAP/STAP*		*BCAP*		*Others*		*Total*	
	Units	*Amount*	*Units*	*Amount*	*Units*	*Amount*	*Units*	*Amount*	*Units*	*Amount*
1999-00	1337	80.55 (73.42)	157	16.13 (14.70)	57	5.19 (4.73)	90	7.84 (7.15)	1641	109.71 (100)
2000-01	632	73.27 (92.28)	26	2.64 (3.33)	59	2.09 (2.64)	12	1.40 (1.76)	729	79.40 (100)
2001-02	628	210.78 (83.60)	86	15.74 (6.24)	40	9.60 (3.81)	114	16.00 (6.35)	686	252.12 (100)
2002-03	818	132.83 (78.42)	119	11.74 (6.93)	31	5.11 (3.01)	116	19.71 (11.64)	1084	169.39 (100)
2003-04	311	164.01 (61.83)	232	36.09 (13.61)	31	6.42 (2.42)	224	58.74 (22.14)	798	265.26 (100)

Note: Figures in the parentheses indicate percentage to total.
Source: Annual reports of RGB, Cuddapah

Table 13
SHG Linkage and Loans Disbursed and Outstanding

(Rs. in lakhs)

Year	*SHGs Linked During the Year*	*Loans Disbursed*	*Loans Outstanding*
1999-00	275	52.89	35.50
2000-01	1820	354.63	271.59
2001-02	2544	619.52	595.56
2002-03	4058	963.56	1036.11
2003-04	7753	2099.93	2198.08

Source: Annual Reports of RGB, Cuddapah.

Recovery Performance

Recovery is an important component upon which the success and the prosperity of the bank depend. A higher degree of recovery would lead the bank on the path of the development. A poor performance of recovery has an adverse impact on the bank. The problem of overdues is, however, not a new one. It is a chronic disease troubling the banks for many years[6]. Poor recovery of loans reduces the lending capacity of the bank and the prosperity and profitability of the bank may be affected. Conversely proper recovery of loans and low amount of overdues inspire the bank to undertake more developmental activities by financing in the area of its operation. Recovery performance is shown in Table 14.

Table 14
Recovery Performance of RGB, Cuddapah

Rs in lakhs)

Year	*Total Advances Outstanding*	*Demand for Recovery*	*Recovery*	*Over dues*	*Recovery Performance -%*
1998-99	24163.14	11746.17	6116.73	5629.44	52.00
1999-2k	26308.81	17410.05	9585.80	7824.25	55.00
2000-01	31344.86	13762.58	8684.62	5077.96	63.00
2001-02	37992.58	21051.54	13160.26	7391.28	65.00
2002-03	45118.30	21368.76	14384.32	6984.44	67.31
2003-04	56942.30	30489.26	19993.19	10496.07	66.00

Source: Annual reports of RGB, Cuddapah

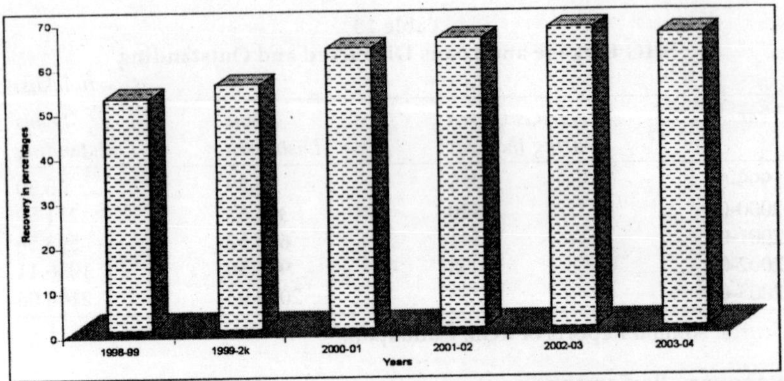

Figure 5: Recovery Performance of RGB

It is obvious that the percentage of recovery had increased from 52 per cent in 1998-99 to 66 per cent 2003-2004. The percentage of recovery was more than 50 per cent in all the years under study. It is inferred that the recovery performance of the bank has been increasing gradually.

To ascertain the rate of increase/decrease in the recovery performance of RGB, trend values are calculated. The results of trend reveal that the recovery performance of RGB is increasing year after year with the rate of 1.56

Sector-Wise Classification of Recovery Performance of RGB

RGB's advances can be mainly classified into priority and non-priority sector. Priority sector consists of farm sector such as crop production, agriculture term loans and loans for agriculture- allied activities and non-farm sector such as rural artisans, transport operators, retail trade, SHGs and others.

Table 15 reveals the information regarding the sector-wise classification of recovery performance of RGB. The recovery performance in both priority and non-priority sectors recorded more or less equal during the study period except in the year 2003-04. In 1998-99, the recovery performance in non- priority sector was 51, which gradually augmented to 76.0 per cent in 2003-04. In the case of priority sector also, it increased from 52 per cent in 1998-99 and reached to 66 per cent in 2003-04. It is, further, observed that though there is an increase in the

Table 15

Sector Wise Classification of Recovery Performance of RGB, Cuddapah

(Rs.in lakhs)

Year	*Priority Sector*			*Non-Priority Sector*			*Total*		
	Demand for Recovery	*Recovery*	*% of Recovery*	*Demand for Recovery*	*Recovery*	*% of Recovery*	*Demand for Recovery*	*Recovery*	*% of Recovery*
1998-99	9324.19	4888.18	52	2421.98	1228.55	51	11746.17	6116.73	52.00
1999-2k	15087.02	8319.74	55	1323.03	1266.06	55	17410.05	9585.80	55.00
2000-01	11255.22	7070.78	63	1959.32	1071.56	55	13762.58	8684.62	63.00
2001-02	18226.68	11694.04	64	1955.27	1243.87	64	21051.54	13160.26	65.00
2002-03	18384.15	12051.09	66	1928.07	1350.64	70	21368.76	14384.32	67.31
2003-04	21248.67	12098.13	57	2206.69	1667.81	76	30489.26	19993.19	66.00

Source: Annual reports of RGB, Cuddapah.

percentages of recovery in priority and non priority-sectors, recovery performance is impressive in non-priority-sector when compared to the priority sector.

The students' 't' test is applied for assessing the recovery performance in between the priority sector and non-priority sector advances. The formulated hypothesis is that there is no significant difference between the recovery performance of priority sector and non-priority sector advances. The 't' test results reveal that the hypotheses is accepted since the 't' Table value (2.015) is more than 't' calculated value (0.632). It is also gratifying to note that the inferences drawn already have synchronized with the statistical results.

Recovery Measures

In order to bring down overdues, the bank had initiated the following measures such as; [7]

- allocation of branch-wise quarterly recovery targets;
- prompt serving of notices and maintaining regular contacts with borrowers;
- conduction of bi-monthly recovery review meetings at various centers involving clusters of branches in the area, to take stock of the situation and to suggest the course of action to improve the recoveries;
- analysis of loan accounts of chronic defaulters and initiating appropriate action;
- initiation of legal action and speeding up of the process;
- auctioning of jewelries in case of overdues in jewel loans;
- availing of the services of Vikas Volunteer Vahini clubs, Farm Information Exchange clubs and other well-wishers of the bank to bring about a better recovery climate;
- serving of notices from head offices to the chronic defaulters and also to the borrowers who much utilised loans;

- streamlining the information system on recoveries;
- introduction of a scheme of awards for recognising high level of recovery performance by all cadres of staff;
- Continued publication of monthly "Recovery Bulletin" by highlighting recovery performance of branches, areas and individual staff members to infuse competitive spirit among them.

Refinance Availed By RGB

RGB is being financed by three institutions viz., NABARD, Syndicate Bank, and Small Industries Development Bank of India (SIDBI). Refinance availed by RGB is presented in Table 16.

Table 16
Refinance Availed by RGB, Cuddapah

(Rs. in lakhs)

Year	*NABARD*	*Sponsored Bank*	*SIDBI*	*Total*
1998-99	4963.3 (71.92)	1919.14 (27.81)	18.39 (0.27)	6900.83 (100)
1999-2k	4449.52 (66.49)	2218.35 (33.15)	24.32 (0.36)	6692.19 (100)
2000-01	5038.74 (66.54)	2533.39 (33.46)	-	7572.13 (100)
2001-02	4387.90 (53.98)	3740.56 (46.02)	-	8127.46 (100)
2002-03	6535.35 (35.87)	11682.00 (64.13)	-	18218.35 (100)
2003-04	3173.48 (29.13)	7719.00 (70.87)	-	10892.48 (100)

Source: Annual Reports of RGB, Cuddapah.

It is evident that refinance from NABARD was more during the initial years of the study period, it was declined in later years. Out of the total refinance of Rs. 6900.83 lakhs from all the sources, the refinance availed by RGB from NABARD constituted 71.92 per cent in 1998-99 and tended to decline gradually to 29.13 per cent in 2003-04. In the case of sponsor bank, a reverse trend may be observed in all the years of study. It is concluded that RGB had relied more on NABARD for its refinance facility upto 2001-02. But later, it heavily depended on Sponsored bank for availing the refinance. It is disheartening to mention that SIDBI role was very insignificant.

OTHER SCHEMES OF RGB

National Agriculture Insurance Scheme

The RGB has been implementing the Comprehensive Crop Insurance Scheme (CCIS) through its branches and Farmers Service Societies since 1985. The Government of India has introduced new crop insurance scheme namely Rashtria Krishi Bhima Yojana or National Agriculture Insurance Scheme (NAIS) with effect from Rabi 1999-2000 in the place of present CCIS. As the Govt of Andhra Pradesh have not given consent for the new scheme, the bank has not implemented new scheme for Rabi 1999-2000. The bank had received the insurance claim of Rs.4,878.93 lakhs for the benefit of the farmers from the General Insurance Company over a period of five years i.e., from 1999-2000 to 2003-2004.

Rural Entrepreneurs Development Programme (REDP)

Rural Entrepreneurs Development Programme is being conducted by the RGB with the financial support of NABARD. In this programme, training is given to the rural artisans and other unemployed youth in their respective interested areas like fashion technology, pickle making, juice making, and the like. About 13 programmes were conducted and training was given to the rural poor from 1998-99 to 2003-2004[8]. Most of them were the members of SHGs.

REFERENCES

1. Annual Report (2002-03), Rayalaseema Grameena Bank, Cuddapah, p.5.
2. Annual Report (2003-2004), op.cit., p.4.
3. Report of the Banking Commission (1972), Government of India, p.629.
4. Annual Report (2003-2004), op.cit., p.11.
5. Tanan, M.L. (1993), *Banking Law and Practice in India*, New Delhi, Orient Law House, p.119.
6. Dadchi, C.L. (1977), *Overdues in Farm Cooperative Credit*, Bombay: Popular Prakashan, p.17.

7. Gopal Swaroop (1999), *Advances to Small Industries and Small Borrwers*, New Delhi: Sultan Chand & Sons, March, p.526.

8. Annual Report (1997-98), op.cit., p.7.

9. Annual Report, 2003-04, op.cit., p.17.

5

Impact of RGB Financing on Rural Development

To asses the impact of Rayalaseema Grameena Bank financing in Cuddapah district, a study was conducted by selecting branches from the three service areas of the RGB, namely, Cuddapah, Proddutur and Rajempet. For the purpose of study, five branches have been selected. They are Chintakommadinne (CK Dinne) branch from Cuddapah service area, Mylavaram and Alavalapadu branches from Proddutur service area, Nandalur and Pullmpeta branches from Rajempet service area. An attempt has been made to find out the general impact of the Bank (RGB) financing under different schemes in these sample branch areas of the district. The branch selection is made covering all the three divisions of Cudapah District i.e Jammalamadugu, Cuddapah, and Rajempeta. The beneficiaries were chosen from different branches. To assess the impact of RGB financing on the socio-economic conditions of the beneficiaries, one year period starting with April 2002 and ending with March 2003, has been considered [see chapter-3].

SAMPLE BRANCHES: A BRIEF NOTE

Details of the sample branches are manifested in Table 1. Out of the total five sample branches, three branches namely C.K. Dinne, Nandalur and Mylavaram were established in the year 1977.

Table 1
Details of the Sample Branches

Name of the Service Area	Name of the Branch	Date of Establishment	Human Resource Position				Total
			Managers	Officers	Clerks	Messengers	
Cuddapah	C.K. Dinne	08-12-1977	1	–	2	1	4
Rajempet	Nardalur	02-09-1977	1	2	4	1	8
	Pullampet	07-06-2001	1	–	2	1	4
Proddatur	Mylavaram	20-12-1977	1	1	2	–	4
	Alavalapadu	31-01-1985	1	1	2	1	5
Total			5	4	12	4	25

Source: Official Records of RGB, Cuddapah

Alavalapadu and pullampet were started in 1985 and 2001 respectively. The total staff of all the five branches is 25. Of these, five members, in the managerial cadre; four in the officer cadre; 12 in the clerical grade, are working. In addition, four messengers are also working in the bank branches.

DEPOSITS AND ADVANCES OF THE SELECT BRANCHES

Deposit Mobilization

Deposits of the bank are depending upon the saving capacity and habit of the people. To increase the deposits, banks have to put their efforts to inculcate savings habit among the public. In order to improve the deposits, RGB introduced varieties of deposit schemes such as Fixed deposits, Janbadratha deposits, Lakshmi cash certificates, Soubahagya deposits, Kamadenu deposits and the like. RGB offers attractive interest rates on these deposit schemes ranging from 4.25 to 7.00 percent to attract the rural poor.

Position of deposits is shown in Table 2. All the branches of study area are mobilizing deposits under three heads namely, Demand deposits, Savings deposits and Term deposits. It is understood that all the sample branches such as C.K. Dinne, Malavaram, Alavalapadu, Nandalur, and Pullampet could mobilize funds largely through Term deposits. The percentage of Term deposits to total deposits had varied in between 70.5 and 82.45 over the year under reference. Saving deposits have never exceeded one-third of total deposits. Demand deposits could not cross even three per cent of the total deposits in any branch under study. The reason is that the rate of interest on the Term deposits is more attractive when compared to demand and savings deposits.

Sector-Wise Classification of Loans and Advances

Rural bank finance is mainly confined to the development of the rural poor only. Almost all the people in rural areas depending on agriculture and agriculture allied activities. To realise the goal of modern welfare state, it has become necessary not only to achieve self-sufficiency in matters of food

Table 2
Position of Deposits in Sample Branches

(Rs. in lakhs)

Name of the Service Area	*Name of the Branch*	*Demand Deposits*	*Savings Deposits*	*Term Deposits*	*TotalDeposits*
Cuddapah	C K Dinne	4.06 (1.18)	97.17 (28.32)	241.90 (70.50)	343.13 (100)
Rajempet	Nandalur	22.31 (2.44)	146.95 (16.05)	746.38 (81.51)	915.64 (100)
	Pullampet	2.45 (0.98)	54.25 (21.70)	193.35 (77.32)	250.05 (100)
Proddatur	Mylavaram	1.32 (0.50)	45.21 (17.05)	218.64 (82.45)	265.17 (100)
	Alavalapadu	0.74 (0.52)	32.13 (22.50)	109.91 (76.98)	142.78 (100)
Total		30.87 (1.61)	375.71 (19.60)	1510.17 (78.79)	1916.78 (100)

Note: Figures in the parentheses represent percentage to total
Source: Official Records of the Sample RGB branches of RGB8

and agricultural raw materials, but to achieve highly mechanised agriculture so as to throw up surpluses to be made available for investment in the other sectors of the economy.

Table 3 depicts the information regarding advances to various sectors. The bank finance is mainly classified into two categories such as priority sector and non-priority sector. It is evident that 70 to 90 per cent of the total loans are given to priority sector in the cases of C K Dinne, Myalavaram and Alavalapadu branches, whereas Priority sector was given less importance in Nandalur and Pullampet branches, wherein 70 to 85 per cent of total loans and advances were given to Non-priority sector. The reason is that the beneficiaries belong to Nandalur and Pullampet branches are depending less on agricultural activities. Most of the people have migrated to Gulf Countries for their lively-hood. Some people are doing business and the rest is on agricultural activities. Owing to this, bank finance is also very less to agricultural and agricultural-allied activities in Nadalur and Pullmpet branches.

Table 3
Sector-wise Classification of Advances

(Rs. in lakhs)

Name of the Service Area	*Name of the Branch*	*Priority Sector*	*Non-priority Sector*	*Total Advances*
Cuddapah	C K Dinne	160.11 (73.98)	56.32 (26.02)	216.43 (100)
Rajempet	Nandalur	47.82 (22.34)	166.28 (77.66)	214.10 (100)
	Pullampet	11.75 (15.74)	62.93 84.26)	74.68 (100)
Proddatur	Mylavaram	152.67 (70.09)	65.14 (29.91)	217.81 (100)
	Alavalapadu	505.58 (93.64)	34.32 (6.36)	539.90 (100)
Total		877.93 (69.51)	385.00 (30.49)	1262.93 (100)

Note: Figures in the parentheses represent percentage to total
Source: Official Records of the sample branches of RGB

Purpose-Wise Classification of Loans and Advances

Though the priority sector advances i.e agriculture and agriculture-allied activities are prime importance of the bank, it shall not overlook the non- priority sector advances such as small business, rural artisans, village and cottage industries and the like. Because, overall development is possible when all the sectors are developed. So, bank sanctions the different kinds of loans such as agricards and farm loans, agricultural jewelry loans, general jewelry loans, loans on deposits, education loans, demand loans, loans to Self Help Groups [SHGs], vehicle loans, staff loans and the like.

Table 4 depicts the purpose-wise classification of loans and advances by sample branches. It is observed that the loans and advances to agriculture under the heads like Agricards and Farm loans occupied first place in C K Dinne, Mylavaram and Alavalapadu branches. Especially in Alavalapadu branch, it was 91.86 per cent. Because, 95 per cent of the people in these service areas are depending on agriculture. In Nandalur and Pullampet branches, Demand loans and Loans on deposit stood at second place with 35.41 and 27.66 percentages respectively. Loans for SHGs have not exceeded even 4.00 per cent of the total advances in any branch. The reason is that as the SHG programme was started in recent years and the people are not fully aware of this programme. On an average loans on Agricards and Farm loans occupied the first place in all branches except in Nandalur and Pullampet branches.

PROFILE OF THE SAMPLE RESPONDENTS

Caste-wise Classification of Sample Beneficiaries

The primary objective of the bank is to uplift the rural poor. Nearly 60 to 70 per cent of the rural poor belong to lower castes like scheduled caste, scheduled tribe, and some portion of the backward castes. Development of these castes would lead to the development of the rural areas. To know which caste is given more importance by the bank while sanctioning the loans, the researcher classified the total sample beneficiaries based on their castes.

Table 5 shows the caste-wise classification of sample households. Out of the total 674 beneficiaries, 17 beneficiaries are scheduled tribe while 72 belong to scheduled caste.

Table 4

Purpose-wise Classification of Loans and Advances in the Study Area

(Rs in lakhs)

Name of the Service Area	*Name of the Branch*	*Agricards / Farm Loans*	*Agriculture Jewelry & General Jewelry Loans*	*Vehicle Loans*	*Demand Loans on Deposits*	*SHGs*	*Education Loans*	*Staff Loans*	*Others*	*Total*
Cuddapah	C.k. Dinne	99.40 (45.93)	22.40 (10.35)	2.24 (1.04)	41.20 (19.03)	6.63 (3.06)	0.90 (0.41)	8.15 (3.77)	35.51 (16.41)	216.43 (100)
Rajempet	Nandalur	8.55 (3.99)	32.55 (15.20)	41.31 (19.29)	75.78 (35.41)	5.55 (2.59)	-	9.68 (4.52)	40.68 (19.00)	214.10 (100)
	Pullampet	2.56 (3.43)	18.33 (24.55)	0.27 ((0.36)	20.66 (27.66)	0.93 (1.24)	-	1.15 (1.53)	30.78 (41.23)	74.68 (100)
Proddutur	Mylavaram	115.28 (52.93)	8.31 (3.82)	-	60.12 (27.60)	3.72 (1.71)	-	12.22 (5.61)	18.16 (8.33)	217.81 (100)
	Alavalapadu	495.93 (91.86)	7.55 (1.39)	-	20.39 (3.78)	4.85 (0.90)	-	9.64 (1.79)	1.54 (0.28)	539.90 (100)

Note: Figures in the parentheses represent percentage to total

Source: Official Records of the sample branches of RGB

Table 5
Caste wise Classification of Sample Beneficiaries

Name of the Service Area	*Name of the Branch*	*Scheduled Caste*	*Scheduled Tribe*	*Backward Caste*	*Others*	*Total*
Cuddapah	C.K.Dinne	12 (8.51)	5 (3.55)	47 (33.33)	77 (54.61)	141 (100)
Rajempet	Nandalur	9 (13.43)	3 (4.48)	24 (35.82)	31 (46.27)	67 (100)
	Pullampet	11 (16.18)	2 (2.94)	31 (45.59)	24 (35.29)	68 (100)
Proddutur	Mylavaram	19 (9.55)	4 (2.01)	71 (35.68)	105 (52.76)	199 (100)
	Alavalapadu	21 (10.55)	3 (1.51)	62 (31.16)	113 (56.78)	199 (100)
Total		72 (10.68)	17 (2.52)	235 (34.87)	350 (51.93)	674 (100)

Note: Figures in the parentheses represent percentage to total
Source: Compiled from the Schedule

About 350 (51.93 per cent) beneficiaries are other castes and 235 beneficiaries hail from backward castes. The branch-wise data reveals that, backward castes are more in Pullampet branch with 45.59 per cent when compared to other branches. More beneficiaries from other castes have got the loan from Mylavaram branch. Scheduled caste and scheduled tribe beneficiaries could not exceed 16.18 per cent and 4.48 per cent respectively. It indicates that the bank usually concentrated more on other castes and backward caste. The reason is that, majority of the loans are crop loans and major portion of the

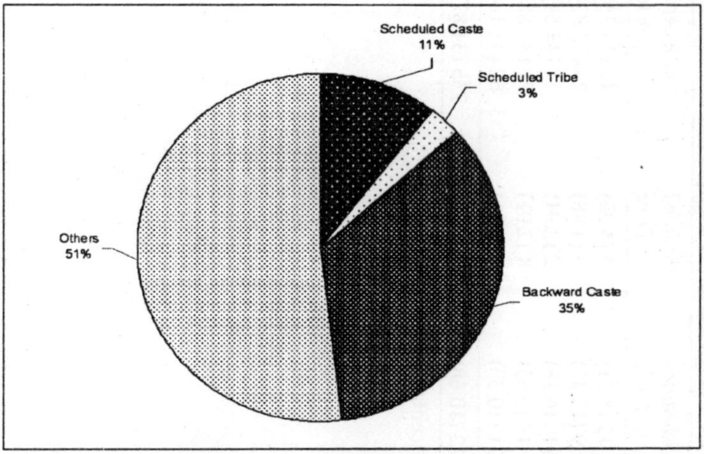

Figure 1: Caste Wise Classification of Sample Beneficiaries

lands are owned by the other communities and backward classes. And the bank also has felt that repaying capacity is more in these categories. Most of the scheduled caste and scheduled tribe beneficiaries have got the loans under special schemes like Scheduled Caste Action plan (SCAP), Scheduled Tribe Action Plan (STAP), Self Help Groups (SHGs), Prime Minister Rojgar Yojana (PMRY), Chief Minister Rojgar Yojana (CMEY).

The 'F' test has been applied inorder to examine the significance of varience in between the sample branches and different castes. Table 6 depicts that the calculated value value of 'F' ratio for different branches is 3.1512. The Table value of

Table 6
Analysis of Variance of Caste-wise Distribution of Sample Households

Source of Variance	*Sum of Squares*	*Degree of Freedom*	*Mean Square Values*	*'F' Ratio (Calculated value of 'F')*	*Critical Values (Table Values of 'F' at 5% level)*
Sample Branches	4335.2	4	1083.80	3.1512	3.26
Castes	13925.8	3	4641.93	13.4966	3.49
Error or Residual	4089.04	12	343.93		

Source: Computed on the basis of data furnished in Table 6.5

at 5% level of significance for V1= 4 and V2=12 is 3.26. It is evident that 'F' calculated value is less than the Table value. It is thus concluded that there is no significant difference between the sample branches in the caste-wise distribution of loans. The calculated value of 'F' ratio in between the different castes in the sample branches is 13.4966. The Table value of 'F' at 5% level of significance for V1=3 and V2 =12 is 3.49. It is apparent that 'F' calculated value is greater than the Table value at 5% level of significance. It indicates that there is significant difference between the different castes in the distribution of loans by RGB.

Distribution of Sample Households by Occupation

Branches of RGB in all the service areas sanction the loans to both priority and non-priority sectors. In all the branches under study, beneficiaries belonging to different categories and occupations have taken the loans and advances. To carry out the analysis and interpretation, respondents have been classified into five categories. They are agriculturists, agriculture labourers, rural artisans, small business and others.

Table 7 indicates the distribution of the selected households according to their occupations. It is evident that out of the 674 sample beneficiaries, 345 (51.19 per cent) beneficiaries are agriculturists whereas 11.42 per cent are agricultural labourers. Artisans and small business constitute only 16.77

Table 7
Distribution of Sample Households by Occupation

Name of the Service Area	*Name of the Branch*	*Agri-culturists*	*Agri-Labour*	*Artisans*	*Small-Business*	*Others*	*Total*
Cuddapah	C.K.Dinne	84 (59.57)	15 (10.64)	17 (12.06)	9 (6.38)	16 (11.35)	141 (100)
Rajempet	Nandalur	15 (22.39)	12 (17.91)	21 (31.34)	7 (10.45)	12 (17.91)	67 (100)
	Pullampet	11 (16.18)	9 (13.23)	15 (22.06)	16 (23.53)	17 (25.00)	68 (100)
Proddutur	Mylavaram	106 (53.27)	19 (9.55)	42 (21.10)	12 (6.03)	20 (10.05)	199 (100)
	Alavalapadu	129 (64.82)	22 (10.06)	18 (9.05)	6 (3.01)	24 (12.06)	199 (100)
Total		345 (51.19)	77 (11.42)	113 (16.77)	50 (7.42)	89 (13.20)	674 (100)

Note: Figures in the parentheses represent percentage to total

Source: Compiled from the Schedule

CHI-SQUARE RESULTS

Calculated Value	*Degree of Freedom At 5% level*	*Table Value*	*Result*
102.39	4	24.996	Reject

Source: Calculated based on the data furnished in Table 6.7

and 7.42 per cent respectively. In C.K.Dinne, Mylavaram and Alavalapadu branch areas, the percentage of agriculturists and agricultural labour is more. But in the cases of Nandalur and Pullampet branches only 22.39 and 16.18 per cent of agriculturists have been provided the agriculture loans. The reason is that beneficiaries depending on agricultural activities are less in number in Nandalur and pullampet areas.. In almost all the branches, rural artisans have occupied second place in getting the loans. On an average it is understood that bank has given more loans to agricultural dependents under crop loans scheme.

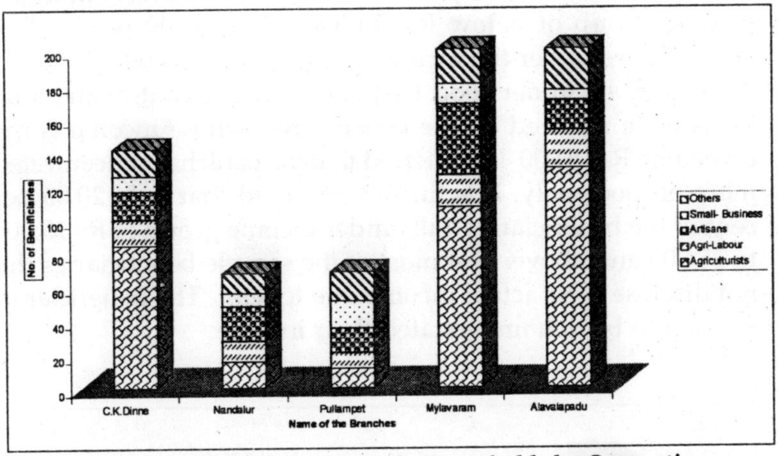

Figure 2: Distribution of Sample Households by Occupation

To test the relationship between location of branches and disbursement of loans to various occupational groups a null hypotheses is formulated and Chi-Square test[1] is applied. Chi-Square calculated value is 102.39. Table value at 5 % level of significance for 4 degrees of freedom is 24.996. Since the calculated value is greater than the Table value, there is a significant difference between the sample branches and occupations of the sample households. Hence, a null hypothesis (*Branch location doesn't significantly influence the disbursement of loans by occupation*) is rejected. In other words, branch location influences the distribution of loans by occupation.

Classification of Beneficiaries Based on the Income

Though the main objective of the RGB is rural development, the bank sanctioned loans to beneficiaries fall under different income levels. In the present study, the researcher classified the beneficiaries in to various income groups ranging from below Rs. 10,000 to Rs. 25,000. The purpose of this classification is to find out which income group could get more loans and which income group was neglected by the bank.

Table 8 deals with the data relating to the households who have received the loans according to the income groups. It is clear that according to the income criterion, out of the total 674 beneficiaries, 46.88 per cent of the beneficiaries fall in the income group of below Rs. 10,000 while 33.09 per cent of beneficiaries under the income group of Rs. 10,000-15,000.

It may be understood that about 80 per cent of the total loans were received by the beneficiaries whose income is not exceeding Rs 15,000. It is inferred that the bank has concentrated more on poor only. It is further observed that only 20.03 per cent of the beneficiaries fall under income group of Rs 15,000 to 25,000 and above. But most of the sample beneficiaries did not disclose their actual income due to fear. The beneficiaries seemed to be rich understated their income.

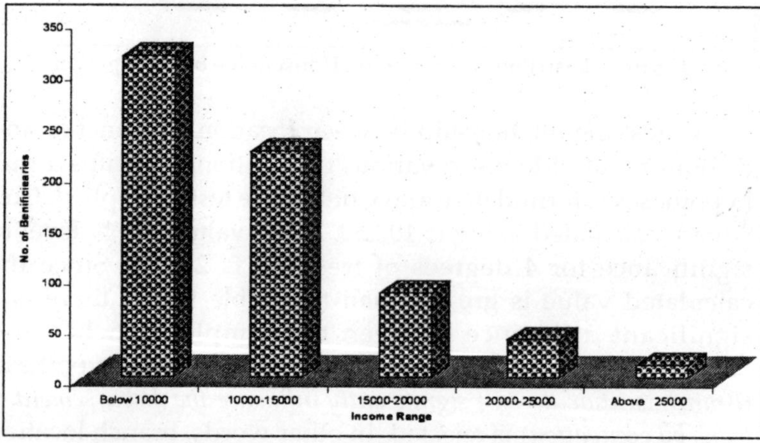

Figure 3: Distribution of Sample Households by Income

Table 8
Distribution of Sample House Holds by Income

Name of the Service Area	*Name of the Branch*	*Income Group*					
		Below 10000	*10001-15000*	*15001-20000*	*20001-25000*	*Above 25000*	*Total*
Cuddapah	C.k.Dinne	71 (50.35)	54 (38.30)	11 (7.80)	5 (3.55)	-	141 (100)
Rajempet	Nandalur	27 (40.30)	18 (26.87)	12 (17.91)	6 [8.95)	4 (5.97)	67 (100)
	Pullampet	32 (47.06)	15 (22.06)	10 (14.71)	8 (11.76)	3 (4.41)	68 (100)
Proddutur	Mylavaram	85 (42.71)	64 (32.16)	36 (18.09)	9 (4.53)	5 (2.51)	199 (100)
	Alavalapadu	101 (50.75)	72 (36.18)	15 (7.54)	10 (5.03)	1 (0.50)	199 (100)
Total		316 (46.88)	223 (33.09)	84 (12.46)	38 (5.64)	13 (1.93)	674 (100)

Note: Figures in the parentheses represent percent to total
Source: Compiled from the Schedule

To test the significance of variances between the various bank branches and between different income groups in the area under study the 'F' test[2] has been applied. Analysis of variance of distribution of sample households by income is shown in Table 9. The calculated value of 'F' Ratio in between the branches is 3.39. The critical value (Table value) of 'F' ratio at 5% level of significance for V-1=4, and V2=16, is 3.01. The calculated value of 'F' in between the branches is more than the Table value at 5% level of significance. Thus, the differences in the distribution of sample households by income in between the branches of different service areas of RGB are significant.

Table 9
Analysis of Variance of Distribution of Sample Households by Income in the Sample Branches of RGB

Source of Variance	*Sum of Squares*	*Degree of Freedom*	*Mean Square Values*	*'F' Ratio (Calculated value of 'F')*	*Critical Values (Table Values of 'F' at 5% level)*
Sample Branches	3468.16	4	867.04	3.3926	3.01
Income Groups	13479.76	4	3369.94	13.1862	
Error or Residual	4089.04	16	255.5650		

Source: Computed on the basis of data furnished in Table 6.8

The calculated value of 'F' Ratio in between the income groups is 13.19. The critical value of F at 5% level of significance for ,V1=4 and V2=16 is 3.01. The calculated value of 'F' in between the income groups is higher than the Table value at 5% level of significance. Thus, the differences in the distribution of sample households by income in between the income groups among the branches are significant.

Purpose-wise Classification of Sample Beneficiaries

Table 10 manifests the purpose-wise classification of loans to the sample beneficiaries. It is clear that out of the total beneficiaries 47.33 per cent of the beneficiaries have taken the loans under agricards and farm loans for their direct agricultural purposes. About 12.17 per cent and 10.53 per cent

Table 10
Statement of the Purpose-Wise Classification of Loans of the Sample Benificiearies

Name of the Service Area	*Name of the Branch*	*Agricards & Farm Loans*	*Agricultural Jewelry Loans*	*General Jewelry Loans*	*Loans on Deposits & Demand Loans*
Cuddapah	C.K.Dinne	54 (38.30)	22 (15.60)	13 (9.22)	11 (7.80)
Rajempet	Nandalur	11 (16.42)	9 (13.43)	12 (17.91)	14 (20.89)
	Pullampet	17 (25.00)	12 (17.65)	7 (10.29)	12 (17.65)
Proddatur	Mylavaram	112 (56.28)	19 (9.55)	29 (14.57)	13 (6.53)
	Alavalapadu	125 (62.81)	20 (10.05)	10 (5.02)	15 (7.54)
Total		319 (47.33)	82 (12.17)	71 (10.53)	65 (9.64)

Contd.

SHGs	*Consumption Loans*	*Small Business*	*Artisans*	*Others*	*Total*
9 (6.38)	-	2 (1.42)	3 (2.13)	27 (19.15)	141 (100)
3 (4.48)	-	6 (8.96)	3 (4.48)	9 (13.43)	67 (100)
5 (7.35)	-	-	8 (11.77)	7 (10.29)	68 (100)
11 (5.53)	-	8 (4.02)	-	7 (3.52)	199 (100)
15 (7.54)	-	-	-	14 (7.04)	199 (100)
43 (6.38)	-	16 (2.37)	14 (2.08)	64 (9.50)	674 (100)

Note: Figures in the parentheses indicate percentage to total
Source: Compiled from the Schedu

of beneficiaries have taken agriculture jewelry and general jewelry loans. This amount may be utilized for agricultural purposes also.

About 2.37 per cent and 2.08 per cent of beneficiaries have received the loans for small business and artisans respectively. About 6.38 per cent of beneficiaries have got the loan under SHGs scheme. The remaining are demand loans and others. It is evident that not a single household had received loans for consumption purposes. This may be on account of the fact that due to the fear of non-recovery, the bank was not interested in lending such loans though the weaker section would need it. It may be said that the bank has concentrated more on the agriculture and allied activities only.

Awareness of Beneficiaries on Loan Portfolio

Table 11 reveals the beneficiary awareness regarding the different types of loans in selected branches of RGB. It reveals that out of the 674 beneficiaries, 65.28 per cent of beneficiaries have the knowledge and awareness on different kinds of loans issued by the bank. This trend can be observed in all the branches. About 32.05 per cent of beneficiaries are partly aware of the types of loans.

Only 2 to 4 per cent of households are not aware of different types of loans issued by the RGB. In the case of Pullampet branch, no beneficiary is found unaware of different kinds of loans.

Sources of Borrowings

RGB spread its branches to cover all the rural areas, still the rural people are striving to avail the credit from different sources other than the RGB, such as money lenders, cooperative societies, friends and relatives and the like.

To know from which source the sample beneficiaries have taken more loans, Simple Ranking Scale[3] method was adopted. The respondents were asked to rank the sources based on the priority of taking the loan, as most important, important, some what important and unimportant. Most important source was given a scale value of 4; important was given 3; some what

Table 11
Beneficiary Awareness Regarding the Different Types of Loans of RGB

Name of the Service Area	*Name of the Branch*	*Aware*	*Partlyaware*	*Unaware*	*Total*
Cuddapah	C.K.Dinne	102 (72.34)	35 (24.82)	4 (2.84)	141 (100)
Rajempet	Nandalur	47 (70.15)	18 (26.87)	2 (2.98)	67 (100)
	Pullampet	60 (88.24)	8 (11.76)	–	68 (100)
Proddutur	Mylavaram	121 (60.80)	73 (36.68)	5 (2.52)	199 (100)
	Alavalapadu	110 (55.28)	82 (41.20)	7 (3.52)	199 (100)
Total	440 (65.28)	216 (32.05)	18 (2.67)	674 (100)	

Note: Figures in the parentheses represent percentage to total
Source: Compiled from the Schedule

important 2; and unimportant was given a scale value of 1. In order to study the relative importance given to the sources of loan, the scale values were multiplied by the corresponding frequencies for each source (Number of beneficiaries) and summed up.

An analysis of the contents of the Table 12 points out certain interesting observations. Among all the sources, RGB is the most important source for availing the loan as the highest scale value of 2376 was registered. Money lenders occupied second place with 2248 points followed by relatives and friends. 4th rank goes to cooperative societies with 1779 points. With 1610 points agriculturists stood at 5th place and the least priority was given to commercials banks to get the loans. It is obvious that most of the beneficiaries have got the loans from RGB.

The reasons might be the RGB could spread its branches to the doorsteps of the agriculturists. The main motive of the RGB is rural development but not profit. So the RGB gives priority to the agriculturists while sanctioning the loans.

Utilization and Diversification of Loans

Development of people is depending not only on sanctioning of loans but also on the utilization of that loan in a proper way. If people divert their loan towards the unproductive areas, the objectives of the bank would not be achieved and development would not be seen.

Table 13 shows the utilization and diversification of loans by the beneficiaries in the sample branches. It is observed that out of the total 674 beneficiaries, 295 [43.77 per cent] beneficiaries among all the branches could not utilize the loan properly. Out of the total number of sample branches, highest per cent (61.76) of beneficiaries in Pullampet branch have not utilized the loan properly. Conversely, in C K Dinne branch, highest of 51.77 per cent of beneficiaries diversified their loan amounts to various other purposes. The reasons like untimely issue of loan amount, illness, inadequate of loan amount, payment of old debts, heavy family expenditure are found important which heavily influenced the household to divert the loan to other purposes.

Table 12
Statement Showing the Responses of Beneficiaries on Sources of Loan

Sources of borrowers	Most Preferred SV=4		Preferred 3		Some what Preferred 2		Least Preferred 1		Total	Rank
Commercial Banks	49	196	72	216	128	256	425	425	1093	6
RGB	463	1852	125	375	62	124	25	25	2376	1
Relatives and Friends	270	1080	210	630	102	204	52	52	1966	3
Money Lenders	370	1480	190	570	84	168	30	30	2248	2
Cooperative Societies	170	680	240	720	115	230	149	149	1779	4
Agriculturists	134	536	172	516	190	380	178	178	1610	5

Note: Figures in the parentheses represent percentage to total
Source: Compiled from the Schedule

SV = Scale Value

Table 13
Utlisation and Diversification of Loans

Name of the Service Area	*Name of the Branch*	*Diversified*	*Utilized*	*Total*
Cuddapah	C.K.Dinne	73 (51.77)	68 (48.23)	141 (100)
Rajempet	Nandalur	28 (41.79)	39 (58.21)	67 (100)
	Pullampet	26 (38.24)	42 (61.76)	68 (100]
Proddutur	Mylavaram	90 (45.23)	109 (54.77)	199 (100)
	Alavalapadu	78 (39.20)	121 (60.80)	199 (100)
	Total	295 (43.77)	379 (56.23)	674 (100)

Note: Figures in the parentheses represent percentage to total
Source: Compiled from the Schedule

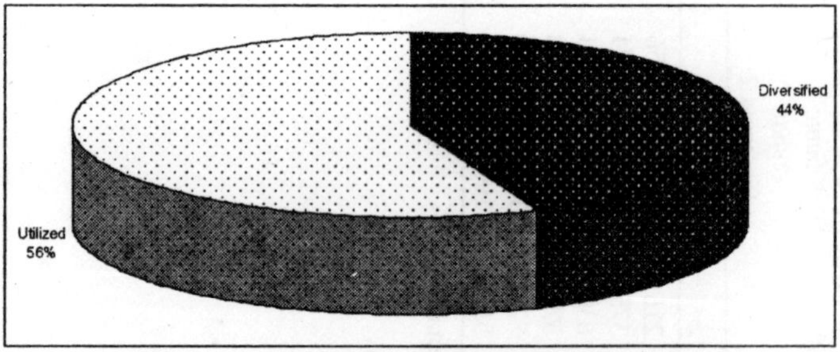

Figure 4: Utilisation and Diversificatin of Loans

IMPACT OF RGB FINANCING ON BENEFICIARIES

Impact on Income

The impact of loans has been assessed in terms of the average incomes. In other words, the average incomes of the beneficiaries from different sectors before and after taking the loan are measured. As may be seen from the Table 14, an increase in the average incomes of the beneficiaries was noticed in all the sectors after taking the loan. But the increment in the incomes is varied from sector to sector. More improvement in the income levels may be observed in the small business sector with 28.47 per cent change in the average income, followed by artisans with 14.77 per cent change. Though there has been an improvement in the income levels among the agriculturists and agricultural labourers, their proportionate change has not

Table 14

Pre and Post-Loan Average Annual Income Position of Beneficiary House Holds

(Amount in Rs.)

Name of the Service Area	Name of the branch	Agriculturists	Agri-Labour	Artisans	Small-Business	Others
		Pre- Loan Average Annual Income				
Cuddapah	C.K.Dinne	12250	8200	9247	15400	9100
Rajempet	Nandalur	9600	7400	8700	13143	7950
	Pullampet	10150	7947	7147	14950	8459
Proddutur	Mylavaram	9400	6200	13400	12100	9429
	Alavalapadu	8650	5900	7500	11200	8149
Total		50050	35647	45994	66793	43087
Average income		10010	7129.40	9198.80	13358.60	8617.40

Contd.

Post-Loan Average Annual Income				
Agriculturists	Agri-Labour	Artisans	Small- Business	Others
13150	8346	10200	21200	10500
9900	8150	9829	14143	8050
11200	8944	8947	19200	8400
9550	7116	14812	18167	10100
9109	6100	9000	13100	8288
52909	38656	52788	85810	45338
10581.80	7731.20	10557.60	17162.00	9067.60
5.72	8.44	14.77	28.47	5.22

Source: Compiled from the Schedule

been satisfactory when compared to small business and rural artisans. Pathetically, change in the agriculturist's income is less than the change in the incomes of agricultural labourers even. The reason is that the agriculturists are completely depending on agriculture. The total family expenditures would be met from agricultural incomes only. They fell in debt in the case of crop failures. This condition might be continued for one to two years in certain times. On an average, an increase in income levels of the beneficiaries with varied proportions may be observed.

Impact on Standard of Living

Standard of living is one of the important measurements to asses the development of the people. In a developing country like India, agriculture plays vital role in upgrading the living standards of the rural poor. Non- availability of timely and adequate credit are considered as important factors for low productivity and it leads to low standard of living. The researcher has collected the data from the sample beneficiaries regarding their standard of living before and after utilization of the loan.

Table 15 reveals the information relating to the standard of living of the sample beneficiaries after the loan is utilized. It is apparent that only170 (25.22 per cent) households have improved their standard of living. About 25.97 per cent have expressed that there was no change in their standard of living even after utilizing the loan also. About 48.81 per cent of sample beneficiaries opined that they have moderately improved. Branch-wise data reveals that the standard of living is improved in Mylavaram when compared to the other branches. Second to Mylavaram, is pullmpet. Least improvement is seen in CK Dinne and Alavalapadu branches. Most of the beneficiaries in Mylavaram, Pullampet and Nandalur are artisans and also depending on small businesses. They could improve their income levels. But in the cases of C K Dinne and Alavalapadu branches, beneficiaries depend on agriculture. They could not develop adequately.

Table 15
Standard of Living of the Sample Beneficiaries after Utilizing the Loan

Name of the Service Area	*Name of the Branch*	*Improved*	*Moderately Increased*	*Remain Unchanged*	*Total*
Cuddapah	C.K.Dinne	22 (15.60)	78 (55.32)	41 (29.08)	141 (100)
Rajempet	Nandalur	20 (29.85)	30 (44.78)	17 (25.37)	67 (100)
	Pullampet	21 (30.88)	28 (41.18)	19 (27.94)	68 (100)
Proddatur	Mylavaram	70 (35.18)	87 (43.72)	42 (21.10)	199 (100)
	Alavalapadu	37 (18.59)	106 (53.27)	56 (28.14)	199 (100)
Total		170 (25.22)	329 (48.81)	175 (25.97)	674 (100)

Note: Figures in the parentheses represent percentage to total
Source: Compiled from the Schedule

Repayment Behaviour of the Beneficiaries

Recovery is as important as advance for every financing institution. Mounting overdue is a major problem in cooperatives, commercial banks, RRBs and even for money lenders. Owing to poor recovery, number of money lenders have become insolvent. The recovery of loan is completely depending on the repayment behaviour of the loanee.

Table 16
Repayment Behaviour of the Sample Beneficiaries

Name of the Branch	*Prompt*	*Irregular*	*No repayment/ Poor- repayment*	*Total*
C.K.Dinne	39 (27.66)	76 (53.90)	26 (18.44)	141 (100)
Nandalur	23 (34.33)	24 (35.82)	20 (29.85)	67 (100)
Pullampet	28 (41.18)	26 (38.23)	14 (20.59)	68 (100)
Mylavaram	99 (49.75)	51 (25.63)	49 (24.62)	199 (100)
Alavalapadu	49 (24.62)	89 (44.72)	61 (30.66)	199 (199)
Total	238 (35.31)	266 (39.47)	170 (25.22)	674 (100)

Note: Figures in the parentheses represent percentage to total
Source: Compiled from the Schedule

Repayment behaviour of sample beneficiaries in select branches is shown in Table 16. The repayment behaviour is classified into three heads such as Prompt repayment, irregular repayment and poor- repayment or no-repayment. Out of the total sample beneficiaries, 35.31 per cent of beneficiaries are repaying their loan amount promptly with in the due date. About 39.47 per cent of beneficiaries are also repaying their due amounts, but they are irregular. About 25.22 per cent are very poor in repaying the dues and, if possible they are ready to escape from repaying the loans also. Branch-wise analysis reveals that the beneficiaries belong to Mylavaram branch stood at first place in repaying the dues, and the recovery is poor in Alavalapadu branch when compared to other branches under the study area. Cultivation in Alavalapadu branch area is completely depending on seasonal rainfall. Heavy crop failures are observed due to uneven rainfall in this area, and also most of the loans in Alavalapadu are farm loans. Owing to this reason, recovery is poor in Alavalapadu branch.

To test the significance of variance between the sample branches with regard to repayment behaviour of the sample beneficiaries 'F' test[4] has been applied.

Table 17
Analysis of Variance of Repayment Behaviour of Sample Households in the Sample Branches of RGB

Source of Variance	*Sum of Squares*	*Degree of Freedom*	*Mean Square Values*	*'F' Ratio (Calculated Value of F)*	*Critical Values (Table Values of F at 5% level)*
Sample Branches	5780.27	4	1445.067	3.6914	3.48
Error or Residual	4089.04	8	255.5650		

Source: Computed on the basis of data furnished in Table 6.16

Table 17 shows that 'F' calculated value is 3.6914 and table value at 5% level of significance is 3.48. Then calculated value of 'F' is greater than the Table value at 5% level of significance. Thus, the null hypothesis is rejected. It is concluded that there is a significant difference between the branches concerning the repayment behaviour of the sample beneficiaries.

REFERENCES

1. Oskar Kampthorne (1974), *The Design and Analysis of Experiments*, New Delhi: Willey Eastern Pvt Ltd., pp. 98-103.

2. Ibid.
3. Krishna Swami, *O.R.* (1993), *Methods of Research in Social Science*, Bombay: Hymalaya Publishing House, pp.297-298.
4. Oskar Kampthorne, op.cit., pp.98-103

6

Problems of the Beneficiaries vis-a-vis Bank Officials

The problems confronted by the beneficiaries and officials of RGB, Cuddapah, in financing the rural poor are identified and presented in this chapter. The problems are plenty. The researcher in the course of field survey has elicited the opinions from the borrower/respondents and Bank official respondents. An earnest attempt is made to highlight the every conceivable problem of considerable magnitude in this regard. The discussion is divided into two parts. Part one deals with the problems of beneficiaries of Rayalaseema Grameena Bank (RGB) while the second part problems encountered by Bank officials concerned.

Several agencies supplying rural credit have also not emerged upto the expectations of the villagers and therefore, the needs of the villagers have not been met adequately. Illiteracy and ignorance, innocence, lack of ambition, dynamism and innovativeness, fear of complex and the like, are also responsible to a large extent for the lopsided development of the rural sector.

PART – I

PROBLEMS OF BENEFICIARIES

A plethora of problems confronted by the beneficiaries are discussed:

Delay in Sanctioning and Disbursement of Loans

One common notion entertained by several critics on agricultural financing and rural development in India is that very lofty aims, objects, purposes, goals, philosophy and programmes are proclaimed from housetops by various spokes men[1]. Needy people are not able to get the required assistance of funds well in time because of too many formalities to be complied with and the procedural wrangles involved in the screening of applications, sanctions and disbursements.

This type of delay has been less in the case of crop loans. But in the case of other loans for small business, loans for tools and equipments for rural artisans, loans for small scale industries, the procedure is very un-adoptive. The Bank officials evaluate the expected returns from the business, viability of the business, and they require proper security also. Fulfilling of those requirements is becoming burden on the part of some rural poor.

Table 1 depicts the responses of beneficiaries concerning delay in sanctioning the loans. It is evident that out of the total beneficiaries, 38.28 per cent of beneficiaries stated that there is a delay in sanctioning the loans. Out of the five sample branches, the problem of delay in sanctioning the loan is more in Mylavaram, Nandalur and Pullampet branch areas as the highest of 49.75, 47.76 and 41.18 percentages are registered respectively.

Table 1
Delay in Sanctioning and Disbursement of Loans

Name of the Service Area	*Name of the Branch*	*No. of Respondents*	*Total Sample Beneficiaries*	*% to Total*
Cuddapah	C.K. dinne	42	141	29.79
Rajempet	Nandalur	32	67	47.76
	Pullampet	28	68	41.18
Proddutur	Mylavaram	99	199	49.75
	Alavalapadu	57	199	28.64
Total	258	674	38.18	

Source: Compiled from the Schedule

Alavalapadu branch registered the least percentage of 28.64. The reason is that RGB gives priority to the crop loans when compared to other loans. Bank will not delay while sanctioning the crop loans. As there are more crop loans in Alavalapadu and C K Dinne branches, the problem of delay is less. In the case of Mylavaram, Nandalur and Pullapet branches, loans other than crop loans are more. So delay might be there while sanctioning the loans. It is inferred that crop loans are provided liberally to the beneficiaries on target oriented basis. There exist less procedural delays in providing the crop loans. In the case of other loans, RGB's officials should observe the viability and survival of the ventures. Therefore, inordinate delays would take place while sanctioning the loans.

Inadequate Amount of Loan

The other problem spell out by the most of the beneficiaries is inadequacy of loan. According to the bank records as well as beneficiaries responses, most of the loans are crop loans. The procedure to be followed for availing the crop loan is easy when compared to the other loans except the loans on jewelry and gold. But the loan amount sanctioned by the bank is inadequate. The farmer is again approaching the money lenders for raising the loans for the purpose of cultivation

Table 2 shows the responses of sample beneficiaries regarding the adequacy of loan amount. The responses of the beneficiaries are classified into three categories based on the intensity of the problem, such as adequate, moderate and inadequate. It is obvious that out of the total sample beneficiaries, 50.74 per cent of beneficiaries expressed that the loan amount is moderate. About 29.08 per cent of respondents said that the loan amount is inadequate while, only 20.18 per cent of respondents said that the loan amount is adequate. Though the rural banks and cooperative banks are providing agriculture finance, still respondents are borrowing money from friends, relatives to meet their immediate agriculture financial needs. As far as branches are concerned, a highest of 32.84 per cent of sample beneficiaries in Nandalur, and the lowest of 23.53 per cent in Pullampet branch areas, opined that the loan amount is inadequate when compared to other branches under study area. More than 50 per cent of beneficiaries in C K Dinne, Mylavarm and Alavalapadu have felt that the loan amount is moderate only.

Table 2
Beneficiary Response on Adequacy of Loan Amount

Name of the Service Area	*Name of the Branch*	*Adequate*	*Moderate*	*In- adequate*	*Total*
Cuddapah	C.K. dinne	22 (15.60)	74 (52.48)	45 (31.92)	141 (100)
Rajempeta	Nandalur	26 (38.80)	19 (28.36)	22 (32.84)	67 (100)
Pullampet		23 (33.82)	29 (42.65)	16 (23.53)	68 (100)
Proddutur	Mylavaram	46 (23.11)	102 (51.26)	51 (25.63)	199 (100)
Alavalapadu		19 (9.55)	118 (59.30)	62 (31.15)	199 (100)
Total		136 (20.18)	342 (50.74)	196 (29.08)	674 (100)

Note: Figures in the parentheses indicate percentage to total

Source: Compiled from the Schedule

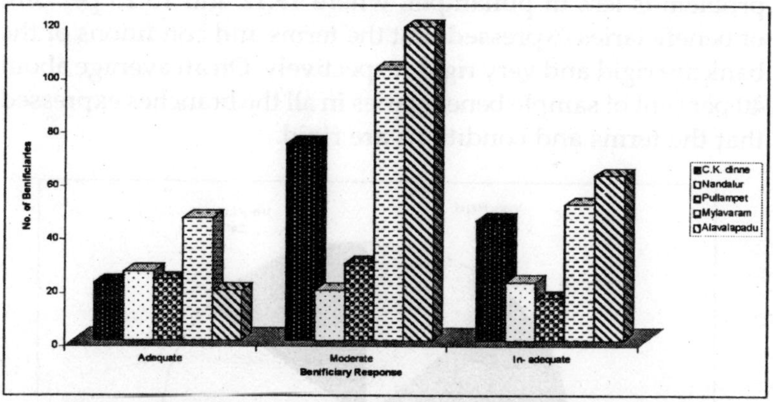

Figure 1: Beneficiary Response on Adequacy of Loan Amount

Terms and Conditions

Some critics opine that there are too many formalities to be complied with, while taking the loans from the banks, and these rigid rules are not conducive for the liberal extension of credit facilities to the really needy, genuine and poor borrowers in rural areas. Some of the sample beneficiaries responded that the farmers, who have access and close touch with the bank officials, are getting the loans easily with out any risk. But, for the poor, maintain close touch with the bank is difficult. For them, following the bank procedures and getting the loans is also a major problem.

Table-3 shows the beneficiary response regarding the terms and conditions followed by the sample branches. The responses are classified into very liberal, liberal, rigid and very rigid. It is evident that out of the total sample beneficiaries, 45.25 per cent of beneficiaries said that the terms and conditions are liberal and 14.24 per cent of beneficiaries expressed that the conditions are very liberal remaining 40.51 per cent beneficiaries opined that the terms and conditions are rigid and very rigid.

In C K Dinne branch, a highest number of beneficiaries (33.33 per cent) said that the terms and conditions followed by the bank to sanction the loans are rigid and 9.93 per cent felt that the conditions are very rigid. The intensity of the problem is less in pullampet, where 19.12 and 13.23 per cent of beneficiaries expressed that the terms and conditions of the bank are rigid and very rigid respectively. On an average about 40 per cent of sample beneficiaries in all the branches expressed that the terms and conditions are rigid.

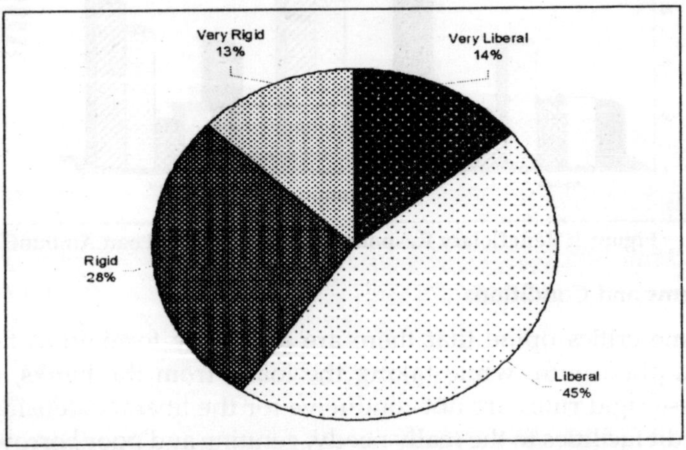

Figure 2: Terms and Conditions of RGB to Sanction the Loan

Table 3

Beneficiary Responses on Terms and Conditions of RGB to Sanction the Loan

Name of the	*Name of Service Area*	*Very the Branch*	*Liberal Liberal*	*Rigid*	*Very*	*Total Rigid*
Cuddapah	C.K. dinne	12 (8.51)	68 (48.23)	47 (33.33)	14 (9.93)	141 (100)
Rajempet	Nandalur	18 (26.87)	23 (34.33)	21 (31.34)	5 (7.46)	67 (100)
	Pullampet	11 (16.18)	35 (51.47)	13 (19.12)	9 (13.23)	68 (100)
Proddutur	Mylavaram	20 (10.05)	101 (50.76)	49 (24.62)	29 (14.57)	199 (100)
	Alavalapadu	35 (17.59)	78 (39.20)	56 (28.14)	30 (15.07)	199 (100)
Total		96 (14.24)	305 (45.25)	186 (27.60)	87 (12.91)	674 (100)

Note: Figures in the parentheses indicate percentage to total
Source: Compiled from the Schedules

Problem of Technical and Legal Assistance

Survival of the present day business is depending not only on effective use of finance but also on effective, innovative and qualitative production. It is possible through the use of proper technology and research. In agriculture sector also, use of innovative technology and equipments became mandatory to get the maximum yield. Lack of technical, marketing and legal assistance is really a serious problem facing by the beneficiaries. All most all the beneficiaries reported negatively to a question "Are you getting any technical and legal assistance in addition to financial assistance form the bank?" Especially in the case of agriculture sector, all the sample respondents are following only the traditional methods of cultivation only.

Table 4 depicts the information regarding the beneficiary response on technical assistance by RGB.

Table 4
Beneficiary Response Regarding the Technical Assistance by the RGB

Name of the Service Area	*Name of the Branch*	*Technical Assistance Provided*	*Total*
Cuddapah	C.K. dinne	No	141
Rajempet	Nandalur	No	67
	Pullampet	No	68
Proddutur	Mylavaram	No	199
	Alavalapadu	No	199
Total	No	674	

Source: Compiled from the Schedule

It is inferred that all the beneficiaries of all the branches expressed that the bank has not provided any technical assistance. It means the bank is not concentrating on providing the technical assistance to the beneficiaries.

Diversification of Credit

Financial crisis is the common feature of the rural poor. The loan amount may not be used for the purpose for which it is sanctioned. This has become common characteristic in the rural credit scene. In some cases, bank loans are used to repay the private loans. In some other cases, loan amounts are used for some occasions like marriages, ceremonies and the like. Few respondents told that loan amount is used for health purpose also. Most of the crop loans are used for different purposes. Because of untimely sanction and inadequate amount of loan by bank, the respondents are diversifying the credit to different other purposes.

Most of the beneficiaries have more than one reason for the diversification of loan amount. Therefore, to know which reason influenced them more to divert the loan, Simple Ranking Scale Method[1] was adopted. The respondents were asked to rank the reasons as Most important, Important, Some what important and Unimportant. Most important was given a scale value of 4; Important 3; Some what important 2; and Unimportant 1. In order to study the relative importance given to the reasons, for each reason, the scale values were multiplied by the corresponding frequencies (Number of respondents) and summed up.

Table 5 manifests the reasons for diversitifcation of credit by the beneficiaries. The main reasons include repayment of old debts, family expenses, social obligations, and medical expenses. It is evident that family expenses tops among the reasons as specified followed by repayment of old debts, social obligation and medical expenses. It may be said that the beneficiaries are diversifying major portion of loans towards family expenses. However it is gratifying to note that some portion of loans were used to repay the old debts.

Problem of Cooperation

Cooperation from the bank official is essential for availing loans from the bank by the rural poor. Though the main objective of rural banks is rural development, the banks are giving priority to the viable projects to sanction the loans. Banks are seeking for proper security to sanction the loan. Illiterate rural poor is not getting proper cooperation from bank. About 40 per cent of the respondents opined that the bank employees are working mechanically, without having any intention to serve

Table 5

Reasons for Diversification of Credit by the Beneficiaries

Reasons	*Most Important* S.V=4		*Important* 3		*Some What Important* 2		*Un Important* 1		*Total*	*Rank*
Repayment of old Debts	40	160	52	156	63	126	15	15	457	2
Family Expenses	62	248	33	99	49	98	26	26	471	1
Social obligations	25	100	41	123	52	104	42	42	369	3
Medical Expenses	18	72	39	117	44	88	69	69	346	4

Note: S.V = Scale Value
Source: Compiled from the Schedule

the basic objective of bank. Beneficiary response on cooperation of the bank officials is shown in Table 6.

It is clear from the Table 6, that out of 674 sample beneficiaries, about 13.20 per cent of beneficiaries viewed that the bank officials are not cooperating well while 23.59 per cent of beneficiaries opined that there is minimum cooperation when they approach for the loan. In the case of the sample branches, 21.11 per cent of the beneficiaries in Alavalapadu expressed that the bank officials are not cooperative. In pullampet branch, about 30.88 percent of beneficiaries said that there is a moderate cooperation from the bank officials. The problem of cooperation is high in this branch.

It, is, further observed that only 29.53 per cent of total beneficiaries from all the branches felt that the bank officials are very cooperative. But, the intensity of the problem has varied from branch to branch.

Consumption Credit

It is very clear that certain amount of credit is also needed for consumption purpose. In the case of agriculture sector, the farm and family are integrated and both cannot be separated from each other for any purpose. One of the neglected areas in the priority sector lending is the consumption credit. Considering the realities of rural India, there is an urgent need for providing consumption credit. This is also the opinion of the Sivaraman Committee, which was also appreciated by the Government[2].

Figure 3: Cooperation of Bank Officials of RGB

Table 6
Cooperation of Bank Officials of RGB

Name of the Service Area	*Name of the Branch*	*Non - Cooperative*	*Moderate Cooperative*	*Cooperative*	*Very Cooperative*	*Total*
Cuddapah	C.K. dinne	12 (8.51)	32 (22.69)	52 (36.88)	45 (31.92)	141 (100)
Rajempet	Nandalur	7 (10.45)	19 (28.36)	23 (34.33)	18 (26.86)	67 (100)
	Pullampet	5 (7.35)	21 (30.88)	17 (25.00)	25 (36.77)	68 (100)
Proddutur	Mylavaram	23 (11.56)	38 (19.10)	71 (35.67)	67 (33.67)	199 (100)
	Alavalapadu	42 (21.11)	49 (24.62)	64 (32.16)	44 (22.11)	199 (100)
Total		89 (13.20)	159 (23.59)	227 (33.68)	199 (29.53)	674 (100)

Source: Compiled from the Schedules

Consumption credit is not isolated from production loan. It should be considered in relation to production loan. If there is no allocation of amount for the family expenditure, the beneficiary may divert the loan amount towards the family expenses. In such cases the purpose of loan for which he has taken may not be surved. The idea of granting consumption loan is that it will provide minimum resources to the beneficiary to survive till harvest season. The expectation is that the loan will be repaid along with the production loan after harvest.

Problem of Marketing

While credit is of crucial importance,.its optimal use depends upon the other complementary inputs made available in time on suitable terms. Recognizing the importance of marketing, advances to agencies engaged in marketing of products of village industries have been included under the scheme of priority sector advances. Marketing is a curial element for developing all the sectors. Major part of the profits at present tends to go to the middle men rather than to producers. Highly dispersed and poorly educated agriculturists, artisans and craftsman do not have much knowledge about the changes in the pattern of demand and prices which their products fetch in the market[3].

Table 7 gives the information regarding the problem of marketing faced by the sample beneficiaries under the area of

Table 7
Problem of Marketing by the Sample Beneficiaries

Name of the Service Area	*Name of the Branch*	*No. of Respondents*	*Tolul Sample Beneficiaries*	*Percentage to Total*
Cuddapah	C.K. dinne	32	141	22.70
Rajempet	Nandalur	41	67	61.19
	Pullampet	49	68	72.06
Proddutur	Mylavaram	119	199	59.80
	Alavalapadu	131	199	65.83
Total		372	674	55.19

Source: Compiled from the schedule

study. It is clear that out of the total sample respondents, 55.19 per cent of the respondents are facing the marketing problem. The branch-wise data reveals that the intensity of marketing problem is more pronounced in pullampet branch area as the majority of the beneficiaries representing 72.06 per cent have expressed that they are not able to market their final produce at reasonable prices. More or less the same trend is noticed in the case of Alavalapadu (65.83 per cent), Nandalur (61.19 per cent) and Mylavaram(59.79). This problem is less in C.K.Dinne branch when compared to other braches in the study area. The reason is that the branch is located very nearer to district head quarter. Marketing, thus, becomes easy in this area. Pullampet area is far away either from Cuddapah or Titrupati. Alavapadu

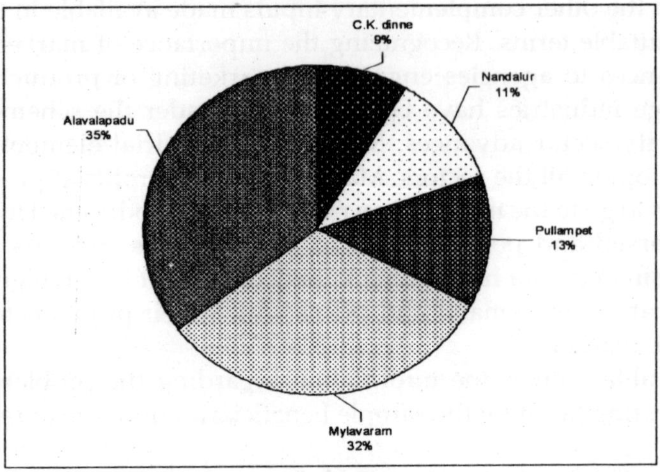

Figure 4: Problem of Marketing by the Sample Beneficiaries

is also a remote area. Transportation facilities are very poor. So marketing the agricultural products is also difficult in these areas.

Lack of Infrastructural Facilities

Inadequate infrastructural facilities, improper planning for the establishment of small units are also some of the reasons for inadequate development of agriculture and rural idustries. All the beneficiaries have expressed that the bank has not provided warehousing facility to store their agriculture produce. Most of the respondents opined that power connections are given for their pump sets. But owing to abnormal power cuts, they could not get expected yield. Arrangements are not made in the matters of supply of seeds, fertilizers and the like. With regard to the servicing of agricultural implements also, the respondent beneficiaries are unhappy. It may be pointed out that inspite of several steps initiated by the Government, the ultimate beneficiaries are not benefited due to lapses in implementation.

Wrong Identification of Borrowers

In fact, this is the problem of banker. But the real sufferer is the household. Because of wrong identification, a person, who is in need of financial help, is not getting the loan from the bank. Proper assessment of beneficiaries is not looked into based on the financial status of the rural poor. In addition to this, Banks often follow biased selection of beneficiaries. Bank may select more than one beneficiary from one family also.

Bank Managers have discretionary power in sanctioning the loans. Using this power, some bank managers sanction loans only to those persons who have deposits in the bank or those who can influence the bank officials. These have resulted in the identification of non - eligible borrowers which has led to frustration and dissatisfaction among the weaker sections[4].

Poverty and Ignorance

The condition of the rural poor, small and marginal farmers, landless laborers, scheduled caste and scheduled tribes is pathetic. Their standard of living is still worse. Out of the 28 crores poverty striken people, 21 crores of people live in rural areas. Their food consumption rate is 20 per cent of the national average[5]. Owing to this pathetic condition, they could not develop awareness regarding different programmes launched by the RRB in particular and Government in general. People are just striving for food and not in a position to know about the programmes launched by the RRBs.

PART-2

PROBLEMS OF BANK OFFICIELS

The researcher has elicited the opinions from the officials of RGB pertaining to their problems in financing the rural poor. To know the problems of bank officials the researcher approached field officers and branch managers of select branches such as C K Dinne, Nandalur, Pullampet, Mylavaram and Alavalapadu. The major problems faced by them are outlined as follows.

Problem of Identification of Borrower

Identifying the genuine borrower is the major problem before the bank officials as the bank officials are not having the close touch with the people living in the different villages. They do not know the income levels, repayment behavior of the people. Identification of right borrower, who is in need of money, is a problem for the bank officials. When the bank officials visit the village to identify the beneficiaries, who are in need of money for their agriculture, small business or other purposes, the real beneficiaries may not be available. Lack of awareness regarding the bank loans, ignorance and innocence in the people are the some of the reasons.

Political Interference

Political pressure plays a dominant role while sanctioning the loans to the rural poor. This is a chronic disease, which cannot be recovered. Owing to political pressures from local leaders, the Bank officials are forced to sanction the loans to the big farmers who are financially sound.

Problem of Recovery

Recovery of loans is one of the important problems of Regional Rural Banks. This is the common problem of almost all the banks. Bank officials could not spend much and more time for collecting dues due to heavy work in the office. Bank officials do not know the time of sale proceeds received by the borrowers. So collection of dues becomes very difficult task.

Problem of Multiple Activities

Bank managers, besides attending the customers, have other various duties to perform such as mobilizing deposits, verifying securities, realizing bank dues, keeping the working of the branches up-to-date, maintaining cordial and healthy relations with staff and customers, attending the meetings, sending replies to inspection reports and the like. Owing to this multiple activities, bank officials are compelled themselves to spend most of their leisure times like holidays in the bank offices. It may be caused to some sort of dissatisfaction in the officials of the bank.

Staff Influence

Staff influences also one of the important problems which mislead the bank officials. A few RGB staff try to influence the bank officials to sanction the loans to their relatives, friends and the like. Bank authorities can not sanction the loan to the right person due to the influence of the bank staff. This is also important problem for selecting the right beneficiaries.

Problem of Verifications of Assets

Though the aim of Rural Bank is to finance the rural poor, the bank has to see the credit worthiness and repaying capacity of the borrowers. To assess the borrower, asset verification is to be undertaken. But assets which are shown to the bank officials may be owned by some other, and temporarily the borrower takes title of that asset only for getting the loan from the bank. This is the major problem for the bank officials to find the real customer.

Problem of Sanctioning the Second Loan

Beneficiaries seek for second loan before repaying the first loan even. In genuine circumstances, sanctioning of second loan goes a long way in helping the banker also in recovering the first loan. Some times the second loan becomes mandatory due to the failure of the first unit. But some beneficiaries tend to apply for a second loan just to repay the first loan.

Problem of Willful Default

It is reported by the bank officials that 20 per cent of the borrowers are wantedly showing disinterest in paying the bank debt. This problem is more in case of the loans under self-employment schemes like PMRY, CMEY, SGSY and the like.

Problem of Technical Development

With the recent technological development in the Banking sector, the RGB. is not cooperating. Computerized banking, online banking , debit and credit card systems are some of the important banking developments in the present technological era. But almost all the Regional Rural Banks are beyond these technical implementations. Recently, computers were installed in bank branches, but Banking system has not yet been computerized.

REFERENCES

1. Krishna Swami, O.R. (1993), *Methods of Research in Social Sciences*, Bombay: Himalaya Publishing House, pp.297-298
2. Khemani, C.L and Balakrishnan, K.V. (1981), *Financing of Weaker Sections*, Importance of Consumption Credit, State Bank of India Monthly Review, August, p.348.
3. Pigmy Economic Review (1995), Syndicate Bank, Manipal: August.
4. Tippaiah, P. (1984), *Working of Differential Rates of Interest Scheme*, Hyderabad : Course Material, NIRD, p.4
5. Venkataraman, B. (1984), *Integraed Rural Development Programme and Role of Banks*, Hyderabad: Course Material, National Institute of Rural Development, p.8.

7

Summary, Conclusions and Suggestions

In India, about 60 per cent of the people live in an atmosphere of obsolute poverty, illiteracy, un-employment and under employment. Attempts were not made up to the desired level to develop socio-economic conditions of rural people. The programme of rural development has, thus become the target of economists, politicians and social reformers. Rural development is an important tool for bringing improvement in the life of rural people, otherwise, all-round development of the country would not possible. Among the various infrastructural facilities needed to improve upon the plight of rural masses, the provision of bank credit is certainly sine-que-non without which rural development becomes difficult. Therefore, bank credit is one of the strategic inputs for successful rural development. The study covers the concept of rural development, an overview of regional rural banks, performance evaluation of Rayalaseema Grameena Bank (RGB), impact of RGB financing on rural development and the problems encountered by beneficiaries vis-à-vis officials of the RGB. A summary of each Chapter is presented in the pages that follow:

INTRODUCTION

Rural development is a driving force of the entire development process and lies at the heart of the National development. It is associated with improving living standards of population, ensuring mass participation in developmental activities and making the development process self-sustain. It embraces all those programmes that touch all levels of human living i.e. agriculture and allied activities, health, communication, employment through village and cottage industries, housing and social welfare.

Rural credit is an arrangement between a borrower and lender, who deploys his capital for earning some interest. Credit is considered an important instrument for agriculture and rural development, which is available from institutional and non-institutional sources. Agriculturists need credit mainly for production and investment purposes. Though there is institutional source of credit, agriculturists depend more on non-institutional sources for their financial requirements. This debt burden passes and increases from generation to generation. In this circumstances, bank credit plays a major role in safeguarding the farmers from the clutches of moneylenders, commission agents, landlords and the like.

REGIONAL RURAL BANKS: AN OVERVIEW

RRBs are the youngest members of the family of rural credit institutions set up in India. The first five RRBs were established on 2nd October 1975, with the object of financing the credit requirements of the poorer sections in the country. The number of RRBs has grown up to 196 with 14,446 branches covering 518 districts by the end of March 2004. The RRBs are controlled and managed by Board of Directors consisting of nine members. The authorised shared capital of RRBs is rupees one crore, contributed by Central Government, State Government and sponsor bank in the proportion of 50, 15 and 35 per cent respectively.

Mobilisation of deposits is one of the main tasks of RRBs. RRBs have strong phenomenal growth in mobilisation of deposits as total deposits had registered at Rs. 56,35,008 lakhs by the end of 31st March 2004. Providing advances to rural people is the important ingredient of RRBs. Outstanding advances of RRBs registered a remarkable rise from mere Rs. 10 lakhs to Rs. 26,11,385.86 lakhs by the end of March 2004.

RRBs provide credit both for priority and non-priority sectors. Priority sector had shared major chunk of the advances (80 per cent). Credit Deposit ratio of RRBs had never exceeded 50 per cent during the years under reference. The recovery performance of RRBs had improved by 13 per cent over the study period. RRBs in A.P also reveals the same trend.

RESEARCH DESIGN AND METHODOLOGY

RRBs are intended to develop the rural economy by providing rural credit and other facilities particularly to small and marginal farmers, agricultural labourers, artisans, small entrepreneurs so as to develop agriculture, trade, commerce and industry in the rural areas. Though the underlying objectives are laudable, the development in rural areas has not been achieved to the expected levels. Hence, the present study aims at tracing out the reasons for inadequate achievement of rural development.

In this context, an effort has been made to review the important studies related to the present study. Since the present study is confined to rural development, the rural branches of RGB are only considered for the purpose of study. Five branches have been selected covering the entire three service areas in Cuddapah district i.e. Cuddapah, Proddutur and Rajempet. The sample beneficiaries constitute 674 for the purpose of study.

The required data for the study has been collected from primary and secondary sources. The primary data is collected from beneficiaries of RGB from five selected branches and the bank officials with the help of structured schedules. The secondary data is collected from various books, journals and various reports of Reserve Bank of India. The collected data has been analysed with the help of statistical techniques such as percentages, averages, ratios, variance analysis, students' 't' test for drawing meaningful conclusions. The thesis is organised into eight Chapters.

PERFORMANCE EVALUATION OF RGB

RGB was established on 6th August 1976 with its Head quarters at Cuddapah under the RRBs Act 1976. RGB is sponsored by syndicate bank. The bank covers entire Cuddapah and Kurnool districts and Markapur revenue division of Prakasam district with 148 branches. The total strength of the staff is 942 comprising of officers, clerks-cum-cashiers and messengers/ drivers. In addition to demand deposits, RGB had introduced various kinds of deposit schemes. RGB could achieve 96 per cent of the targets in deposit mobilisation for the year 2003-2004. It shows the better performance of the bank in respect of deposit mobilisation. The bank has been providing advances to agriculture and non-agriculture sectors. The total outstanding advances of RGB amounted to Rs. 56,942.30 lakhs by the end of March 2004. Of which, Rs. 37468 lakhs (65.81 per cent) was provided to priority sector. The Credit Deposit ratio of RGB had declined from 79.88 per cent in 1998-99 to 68.30 per cent in the concluding year of the study. The declining ratio indicates that the RGB could not use the deposits optimally for the benefit of rural masses. RGB financing also covers the government sponsored programmes like SGSY, SCAP, STAP, BCAP, SHG and others. RGB also initiated some schemes like National Agriculture Insurance Scheme (NAIS) and Rural Entrepreneur Development Programme (REDP).

The percentage of recovery in RGB had increased by 14 over the study period. The recovery is more in non-priority sector when compared to priority sector advances. The RGB is refinanced by NABARD, SIDBI and Syndicate bank. But, more finance is availed from sponsored bank- Syndicate bank.

IMPACT OF RGB FINANCING ON RURAL DEVELOPMENT

To asses the impact of RGB financing in Cuddapah district, the present study is conducted in five branches of RGB namely, C.K Dinne, Mylavaram, Alavalapadu, Nandalur and Pullampet. The sample beneficiaries are categorized based on caste, occupation, income, awareness on loan portfolio and the like. Other caste category occupied major place in getting the loans followed by backward castes. Out of the total number of sample beneficiaries, the share of agriculturists is 51 per cent. RGB sanctioned more loans to beneficiaries whose income is less than Rs 10,000, indicating that the bank provides loans to weaker sections. About 65 per cent of sample beneficiaries are aware of the types of loans offered by RGB and preferring RGB as a main source of finance. Impact of RGB financing on rural development is measured based on incremental income and improvement of standard of living of the beneficiaries. There is a meager increment in the average income of the agriculturists, agricultural labourers and rural artisans. But, there is substantial increase in average income of the small business borrowers. Majority of the beneficiaries opined that their standard of living has improved moderately. It may be said that the rural development could be achieved through RGB financing to certain level, but not to the expected level.

PROBLEMS OF BENEFICIARIES VIS-A-VIS BANK OFFICIALS

The researcher, in the course of field survey, has tried to identify the problems faced by beneficiaries and bank officials. The problems encountered by beneficiaries include delay in sanctioning and disbursement of loans, inadequate amount of loan, rigid terms and conditions, poor cooperation from the bank officials, inadequate technical and legal assistance and the like. Out of the total sample beneficiaries, 38.27 per cent have opined that there was delay in sanctioning and disbursement of loan. The problem of inadequacy of loan amount was experienced by 29 per cent of the beneficiaries. Most of the respondents felt that there exists problems in fulfilling the terms and conditions of the bank to get the loan. All the sample beneficiaries said that there is a need to provide technical support by the bank. About 55 per cent of the sample beneficiaries revealed that marketing for their agricultural products is the major problem. In addition to the above stated problems, lack of infrastructural facilities and wrong identification of borrowers are also identified as other problems. The problems encountered by the bank officials include identification of right borrower, political interference, recovery of loan amount, verification of assets, willful defaulters and the like.

FINDINGS OF THE STUDY

- Deposits of RRBs increased not only in terms of total deposits but also in terms of per branch and per RRB. It means that performance of RRBs in deposit mobilization was commendable in the face of competition with the branches of commercial banks and cooperative banks. The RRBs could succeed in cultivating the habit of savings and banking among the rural masses and they have played the role of social change agents.
- RRBs have been instrumental in channelising the funds into most needed and productive purposes in the rural India. This act has reduced the dominance of money lenders in the rural areas and has changed the lives of many small and marginal farmers.
- The highest Credit Deposit ratio had registered at 46 per cent in 2003-04. The RRBs have failed to lend not even half of their deposits in the form of loans. It shows that the RRBs did not like to bear the risk. They have not been aggressive in identifying and financing the rural productive means.
- A look at the loan portfolio of the RRBs reveals interesting aspects. The priority sector loans occupied lion's share with 75-80 per cent of outstanding advances. The RRBs are on target of lending for rural development. Majority of advances under this category belongs to agriculture and agriculture allied activities. Retail trade financing is next to agriculture loans. Advances to rural artisans and SHGs are very meager. The reason could be that majority of the rural population in India depends on agriculture alone. The other reason could be the low risk involved in agri-loans as they are secured through land mortgage also.
- The rate of recovery was 60.43 per cent in 1998-99 which gradually improved to 73.49 per cent by 2003-04. Non-agriculture sector showed better recovery when compared to agriculture sector. In the agriculture sector, it is the allied activities segment that has dismal recovery performance with 47 per cent. The recovery in short-term crop loans is

impressive at 77 per cent. RRBs, on the whole, put-up a moderate performance on the recovery front.

- The RRBs have started concentrating on recovery of the overdues through various measures that helped them to reduce the mounting overdues from 20.52 per cent to 13.85 per cent over the study period. Still there is adequate scope for reduction in overdues.
- The recovery rate in Andhra Pradesh is slightly less than the national average. The RRBs are undoubtedly performing the assignment in order to bridge the credit gap of the rural areas but they are confronting with a number of problems. The main problems of RRBs are mounting overdues, inadequate profitability, longer gestation period, limited channels of investment, limited staff resources, inadequate state Government support and the like.
- Through a variety of schemes, RGB has been successful in mobilizing deposits from the rural and urban customers alike. The total deposits of the bank stood at Rs 83,325 lakhs by the end of March 2004. Among the total deposits, term deposits had occupied the major portion (62 per cent) followed by savings deposits (33.8 per cent). By and large, it is interesting to note that all types of deposits had reported a rising trend over the years. This trend is most welcome for the bank as it provides not only more advances to weaker sections but also extends funds for long term investments resulting in proper and sound operation of the bank.
- RGB with an objective to change the socio economic conditions of the weaker sections of the society has launched various schemes of advances. Apart from regular crop loans and agriculture term loans, the bank also provides loans to rural artisans, transport operators, retail traders, Self-Help Groups and the like. Besides, the bank has launched various schemes under Integrated Rural Development Programme (IRDP), Schedule Caste Action Plan (SCAP), Back Ward Caste Action Plan (BCAP) and

Scheduled Tribe Action Plan (STAP) in order to drive out the regional imbalances and also to improve the living conditions of the rural poor. RGB also conducts the credit camps in order to provide financial assistance to poor and needy persons.

- RGB also promoted some other schemes such as Women Development Cell (WDC) to monitor, evaluate and formulate suitable lending schemes; Rural Entrepreneurs Development Programme (REDP) to conduct training programmes to rural artisans; and Vikas Voluteer Vahini Clubs (VVCs) to conduct awareness programmes among the rural mass.
- RGB has lent 65 per cent advances to priority sector which is less than the national average of all RRBs (75 per cent). Almost 50 per cent of the priority sector advances are for agriculture and agriculture allied activities. The loan portfolio is equally split between the agriculture and non-agriculture segments.
- It is evident that agriculture occupies major share in total advances. However, the proportion of advances in agriculture is declining. Retail trade segment is relegated to the second priority followed by SHGs.
- Analysis of variance of different segments in priority sector shows that there is significant difference in the composition of priority sector loans over the years. It augurs well for the rural masses that do not depend on the agriculture as the bank is diversifying its loan portfolio to non-agriculture segments.
- An analysis of programme-wise disbursement of advances indicates that the RGB did not follow any procedure to fix the targets per year regarding the grounding of units under any programme. Based on the viability of the project only, it sanctions the loan. It is, further, observed that RGB has given more priority to SGSY when compared to other programmes.
- SHGs are aimed at women empowerment through generation of income and encouraging thrift. Taking the

initiation from the Government, RGB has financed SHGs very actively in the region. The number of SHGs financed by RGB swelled from meager 275 to 9,845 over the study period. The amount of loan disbursed to those SHGs has risen from Rs 52.89 lakhs to Rs 2,099.93 lakhs during the same period. It can be said that the RGB has been evincing keen interest towards the SHGs. Undoubtedly, this trend is paving the way for rural development through the RGB financing.

- The Credit Deposit ratio of RGB is well above the national average of all RRBs in India. But, it registered a declining trend over the period under reference. This is a disturbing trend as the RGB is not able to lend at the same pace of deposit mobilization. Subsequently, it reduced recycling of funds for the productive utilization by the region. A comparison of recovery performance of RGB and national averages reveals that RGB is far behind in this aspect. It is observed that though there is an increase in the percentages of recovery in the priority sector and non-priority sectors, recovery performance is relatively more in non-priority sector when compared to the priority sector.
- RGB has initiated measures like streamlining the information system on recoveries, introduction of a scheme of awards for recognizing high level of recovery performance by all cadres of staff, publication of Monthly Recovery Bulletin availing the services of Vikas Valunteer Vahini Clubs, initiation of legal action and allocation of branch-wise quarterly recovery targets .
- Term deposits occupied prime place in total deposits of all the sample branches.
- Analysis of loan portfolios of sample branches shows that priority sector advances are very high (80 to 90 per cent) in Alavalapadu, Mylavaram and C K Dinne branches and non-priority sector advances are high (70 to 80 per cent) in Nandalur and Pullampet branches. It is in accordance with the socio-economic aspects of the regions. Nandalur and Pullampet regions depend less on agriculture and allied

activities. Thus, non-priority sector had apportioned major share of the advances. Most of the advances under priority sector are agriculture related. Advances by the bank to other sectors like SHGs and transportation are very less. The branches appear to cater to the conventional business only.

- Majority of the beneficiaries (80 per cent) belong to low income group of below Rs 15,000 per annum. It is found that there is no significant difference between the branches in the distribution of loans to the beneficiaries by income.
- It is also found that the location of bank branches has a significant influence on the disbursement of loans to various sections of the society based on occupation. The geographic and demographic profiles of beneficiaries vary significantly from branch to branch in the district.
- An analysis of caste composition of the sample beneficiaries shows that around 52 per cent of the beneficiaries belong to Open Categories (OCs) while the rest backward, scheduled caste and scheduled tribes.
- The bank lending is more towards agriculture sector as OCs and BCs form the largest section of beneficiaries. The reason being the majority of the landholdings belong to them. The SC and ST beneficiaries have availed loans under the special schemes meant for them alone. It may be concluded that the bank has not given significant preference to any caste while sanctioning the loan except viability.
- It is found that RGB is the most preferred source of borrowing of the rural masses followed by money lenders. The commercial banks are least preferred. The reasons might be nearness, ease of getting loan and availability.
- Diversification of loan i.e. utilizing the loan for other purposes than what it is meant for is found to be a major problem among the beneficiaries in the region. The reasons for diversification are untimely issue of loan, inadequate amount of loan, illness and family expenses.

- An analysis of pre and post loan average annual incomes of beneficiaries shows betterment across all sections of beneficiaries. A rise in income is found to be substantial (28.47) in case of small business borrower's followed by artisans. The enhancement in income is too less in case of agriculture labourers and farmers. Uncertainty in yield from crops that are heavily monsoon dependent is the major reason for farmers' malady.
- In the opinion of majority of beneficiaries (75 per cent), there is moderate improvement in their standard of living after availing the loan from RGB. The rural economy in this region is not experiencing considerable improvement as the infrastructure facilities have not grown over the years and people are forced to migrate to towns and cities in search of better opportunities. Though the RGB is financing for the rural credit requirements, it is not sufficient for improving their standard of living.
- Repayment behaviour among beneficiaries is found to be decimal. About 35 per cent of beneficiaries are prompt in repaying the debts while 39 per cent of loanees are irregular, rest of them evaders. Therefore, there is a significant difference between branches concerning the repayment behaviour.
- The problem of delay in sanctioning the loan is confronted by sample beneficiaries (38 per cent). The problem is more pronounced in those branches where non-agriculture loans are more. It may be due to the reason that crop loans are provided liberally to the beneficiaries on target oriented basis. There exist less procedural delays in providing the crop loans. In the case of other loans, RGB's officials observe the viability and survival of the ventures. Therefore, inordinate delays would take place while sanctioning the loans.
- Loan inadequacy is another problem faced by the beneficiaries of RGB. Majority of the beneficiaries felt that the loan amount sanctioned is insufficient. This insufficiency led the beneficiaries to other sources of

borrowing typically money lenders. The exorbitant interest rates charged by the money lenders inflate the cost of funds to beneficiaries and reduce the financial viability of the project.

- On an average, about 40 per cent of sample beneficiaries in all the sample branches expressed that the terms and conditions of RGB are rigid. Though the rate of interest and repayment schedule are more comfortable than alternate money lenders, the beneficiaries felt that the bank terms and conditions are rigid regarding the size of loan, formalities involved and time taken to sanction the loan.
- RGB is not rendering any technical or legal assistance to its beneficiaries. All the beneficiaries have reported that there is no help from RGB in these matters. RGB is concentrating on conventional activities of a commercial bank rather than penetrating into the rural lives with innovative and development-oriented methods. The augmented services are found seriously lacking in RGB.
- In majority of the cases, the loan is used-up for repayment of old debts and to meet the family expenditure. Absence of consumption loan is a contributing factor for diversification of loan.
- It is observed that only 29.53 per cent of total beneficiaries of all the branches felt that the bank officials are very cooperative. The remaining sample beneficiaries are having the problem of cooperation. But, the intensity of the problem has varied from branch to branch.
- One of the neglected areas in lending is consumption credit. It is astonishing to note that there are no consumption loans issued by the sample branches.
- Absence of infrastructural facilities like warehousing, cold storage, power supply and transportation is adding fuel to the fire.
- The farmers are typically small and marginal and they do not have financial muscle to procure agricultural inputs and technically advanced equipment on their own.

- It is observed that there are instances of favouritism, corruption, political influence in the process of identification of beneficiaries, which led to biased selection of beneficiaries. This resulted in frustration and dissatisfaction among the weaker sections.
- It can be said that the condition of the small and marginal farmers and land less labourers is pathetic. Owing to this condition, they are not in a position to develop awareness regarding different programmes launched by the RGB in particular and Government in general.
- The bank officials viewed that they too have certain problems in performing their activities such as political interference in selection of beneficiaries, lack of computerized online banking system and information systems. As a result of shortage of staff in the branches, pressure on their time due to multiple activities like deposit mobilization, sanctioning of loan and recovery is mounting up.
- Recovery of loans, verification of assets and monitoring of loan utilization are becoming difficult for the bank officials as more borrowers are trying to avoid repayment. Willful default is increasing among the government sponsored schemes.

SUGGESTIONS

The foregoing findings of the study have pointed out certain deficiencies and inadequacies. A pocket of suggestions is offered to overcome the lapses for effective rural development through RGB financing in particular and RRBs in general.

- Adequate credit shall be provided for the segments like rural artisans and cottage industries particularly as they have potential to generate employment opportunities.
- There is a dire need to enhance the quantum of lending by RGB so that needy people would be benefited. It also contributes to the adequate rural development. In a nutshell, the credit deposit ratio of the bank shall

be enhanced so as to consumerate the credit with the pace of deposits.

- A specific procedure shall be followed in fixing the targets per year concerning the grounding of the units under any programme launched by RGB. Viability of the project alone shall not be the criterion in sanctioning the loans. Loans can be sanctioned to the needy poor people so that the income levels of the weaker sections may be uplifted.
- The sample branches like Alavalapadu, Mylavaram and C K Dinne shall reduce loan portfolio towards priority sector advances. In other words, the quantum of advances shall be increased to non-priority sector to maintain the parity between priority and non-priority sector advances.
- Loans must be sanctioned and issued timely. The sanctioned loan amount should be adequate. It helps the beneficiaries to mitigate the problem of diversification of loan for other purposes. The officials concerned of RGB shall be very careful towards the timely issue of loans. Bank officials shall take appropriate steps pertaining to the utilization of loans more particularly by agricultural labourers and farmers so that post-loan average annual income may be enhanced.
- Inordinate delays in sanctioning of loans shall be avoided even in the case of non-agricultural loans. To this end, cumbersome procedures prevalent while sanctioning the loans shall be simplified.
- The bank terms and conditions are made flexible which enable the beneficiaries to avail the loan in time from RGB. As a result, loans can be properly utilized for the purpose of which they are meant for.
- RGB shall render technical and legal assistance to its beneficiaries. The bank shall establish technical or legal consultancy cell to help its beneficiaries. The new

methods and services shall be accelerated so as to concentrate on latest activities rather than conventional.

- A monitoring committee shall be constituted by the RGB at branch level. This committee so constituted shall continuously monitor the financial status of the loanees and their repayment attitude so that the problem willful default may be mitigated.
- The loan amount must be estimated based on the latest prices of the inputs to make it more adequate for the purpose. Processing of verification and documentation should be made simple. It makes the bank-borrower friendly.
- Recovery performance of RRBs is very discouraging. The bank needs to improve its recovery rate by actively monitoring and following-up the borrowers. Swift and timely action may be initiated against the willful defaulters. Prompt payment may be rewarded to encourage others also to pay-up. Special recovery drives should be undertaken to get rid of long standing overdues.
- The bank employees need to be given proper orientation and training towards rural development aspect of the bank. They must be proactive in identifying the specific requirements of the people of their service area and formulate appropriate schemes for upliftment of the standard of living of the people in that region. The staff needs to act as change agents and should pave the way to its masses to educate them and instigate development-oriented change among the rural masses.
- The RGB in particular and RRBs in general start taking little more risk to create income generating activities in their service areas. They shall encourage and train the rural youth to take-up new trades that are more current or up-to-date with the modern society. This helps to bridge the gap between rural and urban India

as rural youth will produce and sell goods that are demanded by urban consumer.

- The influences of political leaders in selection of eligible candidates for Government sponsored schemes shall not be entertained. The bank officials shall act with prudence in this matter and implement the scheme with the true spirit so as to reach the benefits to real needy people.
- A separate marketing agency may be launched by the RGB in association with other RRBs to establish a net work through which agricultural produce and other articles of rural artisans can be marketed to fetch higher prices for the producers and eliminate middle men from the rural scene.
- The farmers of the region must be trained in innovative farming methods to get most out of their lands. RGB shall coordinate with Government agencies in organising awareness camps for farmers and also encourages them to adopt new methods of cultivation by providing finance. RGB can also insist on the farmers to follow the advises of agricultural scientists in the matters of crop selection, seed selection, usage of fertilizers or pesticides and the like, by linking them to loan sanction.
- The rural people should be educated about the ill effects of non-recycling of funds so as to make them prompt re-payers. The bank should be rigid on the willful defaulters and at the same time should nurse the defaulters who are in real financial distress to improve their chances of recovery.
- RGB has to concentrate more on the up-liftment of the weaker sections of the society like SC, ST and BC communities. The special schemes meant for these communities such as SC, ST and BC action plans, must be given priority at the time of sanctioning the loan to reduce the imbalances in the society. Empowerment of weaker sections shall be given top priority.

- Non-availability of high cost agriculture machinery is a problem for small and marginal farmers. The bank can group a considerable number of farmers and finance them to purchase agriculture machinery for collective utilisation.
- RGB shall rope-in private agencies or individuals to jointly develop and maintain the infrastructural facilities like cold storage units, warehouses in its service areas to benefit the agriculturists.
- As there are significant differences in the socio-economic conditions prevailing in different services areas of branches, specific schemes that match the requirements of the region must be formulated instead of one-policy for all branches. This customization can lead to efficient utilisation of limited resources for the desired rural development of the region.

Schedule

Regional Rural Banks and Rural Development–
A Study of Rayalaseema Grameena Bank, Cuddapah.

(Schedule for Beneficiaries)

1. **Identification** :
   Head of the Household :
   Name :
   Age :
   Literacy :
   Occupation :
2. Address of the head of the household :
3. Size and composition of household :

Name	*Age*	*Sex*	*Relation-ship with household*	*Educational Status*	*Occupation*	*Annual Income (Rs)*

4. Asset Position :

Lands :

House Property :

Livestock :

Agricultural machineries :

Others :

5. Particulars of landholding :

Land Particulars	*Dry*	*Irrigated*	*Total*
1. Land owned			
2. Land leased			
3. Vacant			
4. Operation land [1+2]			

6. Income on assets before and after utilizing the loan:

	Before Utilizing the Loan [Rs.]	*After Utilizing the Loan [Rs.]*
6.1. Land		
6.2. Hose property		
6.3. Live stocks		
6.4. Agricultural machineries a. Tractor b. Bullocks Carts c. Sprayers d. Other implements		
6.5. Financial Assets a. Cash in bank b. Loans to others c. Deposits d. Securities		
6.6. Business assets		
6.7. Other assets		
6.8. Total [6.1 to 6.7]		

7. Do you know the various types of loans extend by the banks : Yes/ No

8. Are any government officials coming to your village to explain about various rural financing programmes? : Yes/ No

9. Do you know about various rural development programmes launched by the government? : Yes/ No

   9.1. If 'Yes' what are they and how did you come to know? :

   9.2. Under which scheme you got the loan :

10. Specify the different sources of your borrowings :

    Institutional

    a. Commercial Banks

    b. R.R.Bs

    c. Co-operative

    Non-Institutional

    a. Money lenders

    b. Professionals

    c. Agriculturists

    d. Relatives, Friends and others

11. Purpose stated in the loan application :

12. Purpose for which loan is utilized :

13. If loan is not utilized for the same purpose, specify the reasons for diversion :

    a. Untimely issued :

    b. Inadequate Amount :

    c. Misallocation :

    d. Illness :

    e. Miscellaneous :

    f. Payment of old debts :

14. Are the bank officials co-operating when you approach them for loan? : Yes/ No

If 'No' what are the problems are you facing while getting the loan? :

15. Are you satisfied with the existing loan pattern of RGB?

16. Do you feel comfort with the present schemes of rural financing by Bank?

17. The amount of loan sanctioned to you :

    17.1 Did you get the required loan amount?

    17.2 Did the bank inform you that reasons for not sanctioning required amount? :

    17.3 Did you receive the loan in time? :

    If 'No' when you have approached and when you are given?

    17.4. Have you got any subsidy on the loan?

    17.5 Are you satisfied with the subsidy?:

    17.6 Do you feel convenient with the interest charged by the bank? :

18. Have you got any additional employment by utilizing the loan?

19. Incremental income from loan :

20. Status of standard of living of the household after utilizing the loan' :

    a. Remain unchanged

    b. Moderately increased

    c. increased

21. Have you raised loan from other than RRB?

    If "Yes" specify the bank & amount :

    21.1 Have you got any subsidy on the loan?

    21.2 Is the subsidy given by bank reasonable?

    21.3 Is the interest charged by the bank reasonable?

22. Have you repaid the loan within the due date?

23. If loan is not repaid within the due date, specify the reasons

    a. affect in farm production/ business :

    b. Variation in income :

    c. Illness :

    d. Miscellaneous :

24. If you fail to repay the loan amount with in due date, what steps are initiated by the bank? :

25 Any suggestions you wish to offer :

Regional Rural Banks and Rural Development–
A Study of Rayalaseema Grameena Bank, Cuddapah

(Schedule for Bank Officials)

1. Would you give the criteria for selecting the beneficiaries?
2. Are there any guidelines to identify the beneficiaries?
3. Would you mention the basic requirements of borrower for sanctioning the loan?
4. Please specify the purposes for which you extend the loan?
5. Is there any limit to select the number of beneficiaries in one village?
6. Would you outline the different programmes under which you sanction the loan?
7. What are the different ways that you follow to uplift the rural poor?
8. Do you measure the standard of living of the beneficiaries after sanctioning the loan?
9. When the loan is diversified by the beneficiary, would you select the same person for next time also?
10. Are you persuading the beneficiary after sanctioning the loan?
11. Is recovering of loans at the satisfactory level?
12. The steps you initiate to speed up the recovery
13. Please specify the different problems in rural credit development
    a. Beneficiary identification
    b. Recovery of loan
    c. Other problems
14. Would you sanction the loan even there is outstanding amount from the beneficiary?
15. Please offer some suggestions for making the rural development programmes more effective.

Bibliography

A. BOOKS

Agarwal, A.N. (1975), *Indian Economy,* New Delhi:Asia Publishing House.

Ansari, A.W. (1980), *The Changing Villages of India,* New Delhi: Chetna Publishers.

Archana Singhal, B.S. Ysdhsv (2005), *Role of Regional Rural Banks in Rural Development,* New Delhi: Sree Publishers and Distributors.

Arora, R.C. (1980), *Integrated Rural Development,* New Delhi: Sulthan Chand Company.

Balmohan Das, V. Prabhakar Rao, J.V. and Hrushikesavarao, P. (1991), *Rural Banks and Rural Credit,* New Delhi: Discovery Publications.

Basu, S.K. (1980), *Commercial Banks and Agricultural Credit,* New Delhi: Allied Publishers Pvt., Ltd.

Battacharya, S.N. (1980), *Rural Industrialization India,* New Delhi: B.R. Publishing Corporation.

Battacharya, S.N. (1985), *Role of Indian Rural Institutions in Economic Growth,* New Delhi: B.R. Publishing Corporation.

Bedi, H.L. and Hardikar, V.K. (1995), *Practical Banking Advances,* Bangolore: U.B Publishers.

Balsha, H. (1959), *Agriculture Credit in Economically Underdeveloped Countries,* Rome: FAO. Agriculture Studies.

Charanjit and Channa, (Ed.). (1970), *Agriculture Finance in India- Role of Commercial Banks,* New Delhi :Marketing and Economic Research Bureau.

Chandra Kantha, K.S. (1998), *Regional Rural Banks in India,* New Delhi: Anmol Publications.

Chara, D.W. (1980), *Rural Banking for Rural Development*, Delhi: Mac Millan Company.

Choubey, B.N. (1983), *Agricultural Banking in India*, New Delhi: National Publishing House.

Desai, D.K., and Desai, B.M. (1971), *Farm Production Credit in Changing Agriculture*, Ahemedabad: Indian Institute of Management.

Desai, S.S.M. (1986), *Rural Banking in India*, Bombay: Himalayan Publishing House.

Dewan, M.C. (1982), *Agriculture and Rural Development in India*, New Delhi: Concept Publishing Company.

Dubashi, P.R. (1985), *Policy and Performance: Agriculture and Rural Development in Post Independence India*, New Delhi: Sage Publications.

Dwivedi, R.C. (1972), *New Strategy of Agriculture Development in India*, Meerat: Oyall Book Depot.

Elias, A.H. (1967), *Operational Problems of Rural Banking*, Bombay: Vora and Company Publishers.

Etiema and Gilbert, *Rural Development in India*, New Delhi: Sage Publications, 1986.

Gehlawant, J.K. and Kant, K. (1987), *Strategies for Rural Development*, New Delhi: Arnold Publishers.

Giriappa, S. (1976), *Urbanism and Rural Development*, Bangolore: Institute for Social and Economic Change.

Ghosal, S.N. (1972), *Agriculture Finance in India*, New Delhi: Asia Publishing Company.

Gold Smith, R.W. (1969), *Agriculture and Cooperative Credit*, London: Yele University Press.

Guptha, K.R. (1984), *Twenty Point Economic Programme*, Delhi: The Capital Publishing House.

Jain, P.C. (1956), *Agriculture and Cooperation in India*, Allahabad: Chaitanya Publishing House.

Kodesia, J. (1974), *Agriculture Credit in India: An appraisal*, New Delhi: World Agricultural Farmers and Welfare Trust Society.

Krishanamaraju, S. (1992), *Banking Finance and Rural Development*, New Delhi: Discovery Publishing House.

Uma, L.K. (1975), *The Design of Rural Development: Lessons From Africa*, Baltimore John Hopkins Press.

Lal and Mohan (1987), *Rural Industrialization in India*, New Delhi: Deep and Deep Publications.

Mehetha, S.R. (1986), *Rural Development Policies and Programmes*, New Delhi: Sage Publications.

Mishra-puri. (1993), *Structure and Problems of Indian Economy*, Mumbai: Himalaya Publishing House.

Mohsin and Nadeem (1985), *Rural Development through Gevernment Programmes*, Delhi: Mittal Publications.

Naidu, L.K. (1988), *Bank Finance for Rural Development*, New Delhi: Ashis Publisahing House.

Nanavathi, N.H. and Arjaria, J.J. (1970), *The Indian Rural Problem*, Bombay: Vora and Vora Company.

Narayana, N. and Chandrasekhar, G. (1988), *Bank Credit for Rural Development*, New Delhi: Ashis Publishing House.

Pany, R.K. (1985), *Institutional Credit for Agricultural in India*, New Delhi: Ashis Publishing House.

Patnaik, U.C. and Mishra, R.N. (1993), *Rural Banking in India*, New Delhi: Anmol Publications Pvt, Ltd.

Pati, A.P. (2005), *Regional Rural Banks in Liberalized Environment*, New Delhi: Mittal Publications.

Priyan, A.K. (1995), *Regional Rural Banks and Rural Development*, Jaipur: Arihant Publishing House.

Rao, S.K. (Ed.) (1980), *Rural Development in India: Some Facets*, Hyderabad: National Institute for Rural Development (NIRD).

Ravindraprasad, D. (1978), *Co-operatives and Rural Development*, Hyderabad: Osmania University Press.

Sandhu, B.S. (1996), *Banking and Rural Development*, New Delhi: Deep and Deep Publications.

Sharma, S.K. and Malhotra, S.L. (1977), *Integrated Rural Development-Approach Strategy and Perspectives*, New Delhi: Abinava Publishing House.

Singh and Radha Raman (1982), *Studies in Regional Planning and Rural Development*, Patna: Associated Book Agency.

Saminathan, M.S. (1990), *Science and Integrated Rural Development*, New Delhi: Deep and Deep Publications.

Sunil Kumar (1990), *Regional Rural Banks and Rural Development*, New Delhi: Deep and Deep Publications.

Tanan (1993), *Banking Law and Practice in India,* New Delhi: Orient Law House.

Vasant Desai (1992), *Rural Development Programmes and Strategies,* New Delhi: Himalaya Publishing House.

World Bank (1991), *The Assault on World Poverty,* Baktunire: John Hopkins University Press.

B. JOURNALS

Abdul, Dakshinamurthy, M. (1983), *Rich Farmers Garb All Benefits Leave Poor Farmers Lurch,* Yojana, 16, July.

Amerender Reddy (2006), *Productivity Growth in Regional Rural Banks,* Economic and Political Weekly, March.

Balishter (1991), *Performance of Regional Rural Banks–An Evaluation,* Banking Finance, May.

Batnagar, J.S. (1997), *Banks Lending Thumb Support for Industrialisation of Rural India,* Agriculture Banker, Jan-March.

Batteen, T.R. (1988), *Communities and their Development,* Community Development Review, June.

Butt, N and Thorat, Y. (2004), *India's Regional Rural Banks: The Institutional Dimensions of Reforms,* National Banks News Review, NABARD, April-September.

Chakrapani, V. (1998), *Credit Expansion through Regional Rural Banks,* Yojana, March.

Desai, V.V. (1976), *Agricultural Credit,* Eastern Economic, 9 July.

Harpal Singh (1974), *Regional Rural Banks,* Yojana, December.

Kamat, G.S. (1975), *Regional Rural Banks,* Khadi Gramodyog, November.

Karthikeyan, A. (1994), *Rural Development by Banks,* Banking Finance, July 1.

Khemani, C.L., and Balakrishan, K.V. (1983), *Financing Weaker Sections,* Importance of Consumption Credit, Agriculture Banking.

Mishra, M.N. (1987), *Rural Banking for Rural Poor,* Yojana, April.

Narasimham, M. (1971), *National Agricultural Credit Policy,* Economic and Political Weekly, January.

Rao, H.N. (1987), *Expanding Role of Banks in Rural Economy,* The Banker Publication Division, November.

Sandare, A.M. and Freelancer (1997), *Regional Rural Banks Revisited,* Banking Finance, November.

Sarma, R.H. (2005), *Will RRBs Mergers Lead to Efficient Rural Banking,* Business Line, September.

Sambi Reddy, B. (2004), *Assessment and Identification of Rural Poor in India: A Study Based on NSS House Hold Data,* National Bank News Review, NABARD, April- September.

Sathye, M.M. (1998), *New Investment Policy for R.R.Bs: Will it Further Pull Down C.D. Ratios,* Banking Finance, April.

Shete, N.B. (1990), *Regional Rural Banks An Analysis,* Banking and Finance, April.

Singh, Baldev (1982), *Rural Development and National Integration,* Kurukshetra.

Varsheneya, J.S. (1983), *Regional Rural Banks,* State Bank of India, Monthly Review, November.

C. REPORTS AND PUBLICATIONS

Annual Reports of Rayalaseema Grameena Bank from 1991 to 1998.

Annual Action Plan, Cuddapah: Syndicate Bank, 1999-2000.

Government of India Report on Farm Credit, 1973,

Government of India Report of Banking Commission, 1972.

Government of India Report of Banking Enquiry Committee.

Government of India, Development of Revenue and Banking Report, 1976.

Government of India Report on Credit Policy, 1973.

Government of India Report of the National Commission of Agriculture, 1976.

Official Records, Cuddapah: Minerals and Geographical Department.

Reserve Bank of India, All India Credit Survey Report, 1954 and 1957.

Reserve Bank of India, Regional Rural Banks, Report of the Review Committee (M.C.Dantwala Committee Report), 1978.

Reserve Bank of India, Priority Sector Lending and the 20 point Economic Programme, 1981.

Reserve Bank of India, Report on Currency and Finance (Various Volumes)

Reserve Bank of India, Report of the Committee to Review Arrangements for Industrial Credit for Agriculture and Rural Development (CRAFICARD), Bombay, 1981.

Service Area Credit Plan, Cuddapah: Syndicate Bank, 2000-2001.

D. DAILY NEWS PAPERS

The Hindu

Business Line

Economic Times

Eenadu(Telugu daily)

Vaartha (Telugu daily)

Andhra Jyothi (Telugu daily)